M000239151

authentic
homemade
pasta

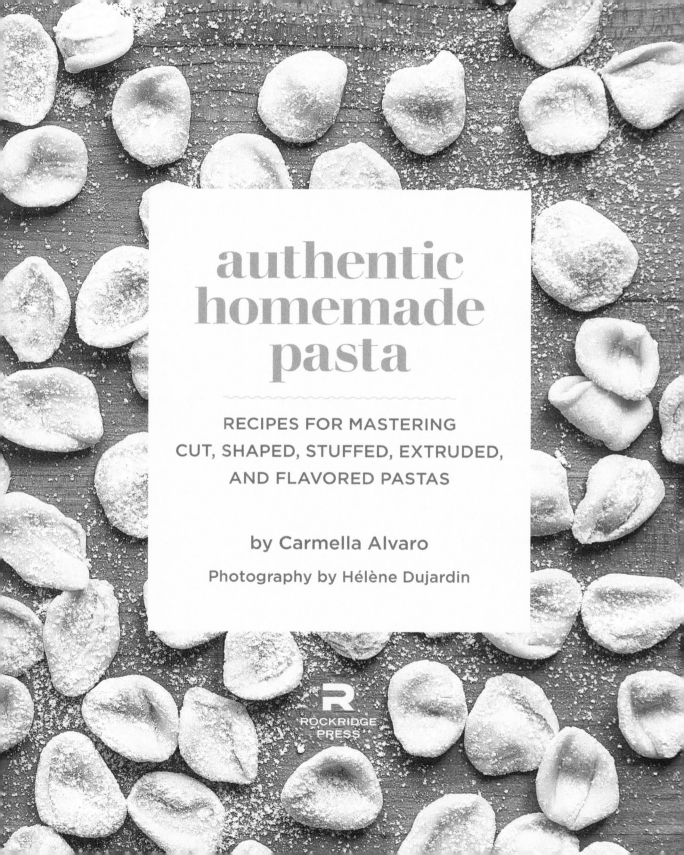

authentic homemade pasta

RECIPES FOR MASTERING CUT, SHAPED, STUFFED, EXTRUDED, AND FLAVORED PASTAS

by Carmella Alvaro

Photography by Hélène Dujardin

ROCKRIDGE PRESS

To my parents,
Giuseppe and Giuseppa Alvaro,
who left everything they knew
to give us everything they could.

Copyright © 2020 by Rockridge Press, Emeryville, California

No part of this publication may be reproduced, stored in a retrieval system, or transmitted in any form or by any means, electronic, mechanical, photocopying, recording, scanning, or otherwise, except as permitted under Sections 107 or 108 of the 1976 United States Copyright Act, without the prior written permission of the Publisher. Requests to the Publisher for permission should be addressed to the Permissions Department, Rockridge Press, 6005 Shellmound Street, Suite 175, Emeryville, CA 94608.

Limit of Liability/Disclaimer of Warranty: The Publisher and the author make no representations or warranties with respect to the accuracy or completeness of the contents of this work and specifically disclaim all warranties, including without limitation warranties of fitness for a particular purpose. No warranty may be created or extended by sales or promotional materials. The advice and strategies contained herein may not be suitable for every situation. This work is sold with the understanding that the Publisher is not engaged in rendering medical, legal, or other professional advice or services. If professional assistance is required, the services of a competent professional person should be sought. Neither the Publisher nor the author shall be liable for damages arising herefrom. The fact that an individual, organization, or website is referred to in this work as a citation and/or potential source of further information does not mean that the author or the Publisher endorses the information the individual, organization, or website may provide or recommendations they/it may make. Further, readers should be aware that websites listed in this work may have changed or disappeared between when this work was written and when it is read.

For general information on our other products and services or to obtain technical support, please contact our Customer Care Department within the United States at (866) 744-2665, or outside the United States at (510) 253-0500.

Rockridge Press publishes its books in a variety of electronic and print formats. Some content that appears in print may not be available in electronic books, and vice versa.

TRADEMARKS: Rockridge Press and the Rockridge Press logo are trademarks or registered trademarks of Callisto Media Inc. and/or its affiliates, in the United States and other countries, and may not be used without written permission. All other trademarks are the property of their respective owners. Rockridge Press is not associated with any product or vendor mentioned in this book.

Interior and Cover Designer: Jami Spittler
Art Producer: Meg Baggott
Editor: Lauren Ladoceour
Production Editor: Ruth Sakata Corley

Photography © 2020 Hélène Dujardin
Food styling by Anna Hampton
Author photo courtesy of Sara Davis

ISBN: Print 978-1-64739-744-9
eBook 978-1-64739-446-2
R0

contents

Introduction

As the youngest child of Italian immigrants from Calabria, I grew up watching my mother, Giuseppa, cook homemade meals with ingredients from my father Giuseppe's backyard garden. After more than a decade of living away from my parents, I worried I was slowly losing my connection to my heritage. So in 2010, I traveled to Italy to take a pasta-making class as a break from the monotony of my corporate job and to learn more about pasta and Italian food. I spent a week in Bologna in the home of the wonderful Tori family of Bluone in Italy Food & Wine Tours, learning how to make and roll pasta the traditional way—by hand. By the end of the week, I was so proud of my perfectly rolled sfoglia—a thin, oval-shaped pasta sheet made with a mattarello, the traditional Italian pasta rolling pin.

When I arrived back home, I thought it would be fun to practice what I had learned and bring my handmade pasta to sell at the local farmers' market. Little did I know, I would turn that sold-out Saturday market trip into a business: Melina's Fresh Pasta in Durham, North Carolina.

One of my favorite parts of the business is to teach classes and share my love of home-made pasta with others. Even more rewarding is when I hear back from students about how they were able to make a pasta dinner for their family and friends. I especially enjoy delving into the regional cooking of Italy and teaching people about authentic Italian food from around the boot.

This book is for people who love creating food inspired by the traditions of Italy. It is my hope that these recipes and techniques will help you become an Italian nonna–level master pasta-maker. In the first part, we will review the craft of pasta-making, including an overview of the ingredients and tools needed to get started. In the second part, we begin with an entire chapter devoted to step-by-step instructions for mastering different types of pasta dough. From there, we will cover a wide variety of pasta-making techniques, recipes, and tips based on traditional, regional recipes from Italy.

Once your flour-dusted hands close up this book, you'll feel confident enough to make pasta on a regular basis and treat family and friends to never-ending bowls and delicious sauces around a table filled with love and happiness—just like the table I grew up at.

PART I

Pasta Primer

Knowing the background and the "why" when learning something new helps you understand a craft better. In the first chapter, we'll start by learning about the science and history of pasta, as well as the basics of making it at home. You'll find an overview of the ingredients needed to make pasta, with a special focus on the different flours used for a variety of doughs. Then pack your bags, because we'll take a tour of Italy with a specific focus on some of the different regions and their distinct pasta traditions. Finally, we will discuss how to properly cook, sauce, and store homemade pasta, and give you some tips on the tools and equipment that will take your pasta-making to the next level. In the second chapter, we'll get into the details of how to make pasta dough, and take you through the steps of kneading, mixing, rolling, and troubleshooting homemade dough.

CHAPTER 1
A Homemade Tradition

Pasta-making is a mix of tradition and science. Italian nonnas may not delve too deeply into the science, but they know the touch and feel of the dough. Their deep understanding of how different ingredients and techniques affect pasta's bite or texture comes from years of practice; yours will begin here. While pasta can be made with nothing other than your hands, a rolling pin, and a knife, we will review some of the essential tools you can use to make different shapes and to simplify the process.

Tagliatelle, page 42

Why Make Pasta at Home?

Once you have tasted homemade pasta, you may end up with a lot of extra room in your pantry where boxes of store-bought noodles used to live. Whether you decide to eat the pasta fresh or let it dry, you'll notice a silky, rich texture with a slight bite that's hard to resist. Making pasta at home also means you can control the ingredients to ensure they are of the highest quality. Fresh pasta doesn't require many ingredients (just flour and eggs at its simplest), complicated techniques, or expensive tools. A few ingredients and simple techniques can create so many variations. This is home cooking at its very best—the meditative process of kneading pasta dough and the care that goes into shaping it, the creativity with the filling for stuffed pastas, and, finally, matching the pasta with a homemade sauce. As little Italian nipote (grandchildren) know, sharing the tradition of making pasta for and with family and friends solidifies your connection to a heritage that can seem more and more distant these days. In so many cultures, deep family connections are forged through food—I am excited to share my Italian version of that with you.

Helpful Translations

Here is a short review of common terminology that will be helpful for both beginners and experienced pasta-makers to reference throughout the book.

Al dente: Al dente pasta is cooked so it is firm when you bite into it, not mushy and soft. My Italian aunts swear that eating overcooked pasta will make you sick!

Al forno: This means "in the oven" in Italian, and refers to baked dishes such as lasagna and cannelloni.

Cucina povera: Literally, "poor cuisine." This refers to a style of cooking that is frugal, humble, and simple, born out of necessity but still delicious.

Cut pasta: Pasta typically made with an egg dough that is cut into varying lengths and widths based on regional styles, tastes, and recipes.

Extruded pasta: Usually factory-made, extruded pasta is pushed through a die to form different shapes. Some small machines and tools can be used in the home to produce extruded pasta shapes like bucatini or rigatoni.

Gnocchi: The Italian word for any type of dumpling, whether made from potato, flour, ricotta, or breadcrumbs.

Hand-shaped pasta: Pasta, usually made from durum wheat flour and water, hand-formed into various shapes like orecchiette and cavatelli.

Kneading: The action of working dough with your hands, or with a machine, to form flour and liquid into a dough.

Pastificio: A pasta shop or factory.

Sfoglia: A thin sheet of egg pasta dough rolled out with a rolling pin; it is used to produce a variety of cut pasta and the sheets for stuffed pasta.

Stuffed pasta: Ranging from ravioli to tortellini—any pasta that is folded over, sealed, and filled with a variety of ingredients, including meat, cheese, and vegetables.

The Food Science

Pasta-making involves the science of developing gluten, a group of proteins that, when mixed with a liquid, hold a dough together. The proteins form a matrix, or net, that affects the strength and texture of dough. In pasta dough, higher protein content means a stronger, firmer dough. Understanding the science behind pasta will help you become a better pasta-maker, especially when troubleshooting a recipe.

The Alchemy of Flour + Water + Eggs

When a liquid (either eggs or water) is added to flour, the two proteins in wheat flour, glutenin and gliadin, combine to form gluten. Gluten gives pasta its bite and ensures it doesn't fall apart when cooked.

How much gluten forms depends on the liquid and the protein content of the flour. Flour with higher protein content will produce more gluten, which results in a strong, elastic dough.

Finely milled double zero (or tipo 00) flour is the traditional flour used for pasta. Its low protein content produces a soft dough with a slight chew and silky texture. Slightly higher in protein and not as finely milled, all-purpose flour produces a somewhat firmer dough than 00. Durum wheat flour has the highest protein content, which means the dough has plenty of structure and the pasta has a firm bite.

Different combinations of liquids and flours result in pasta that ranges from tender and silky to hearty and chewy. Protein-packed eggs add tenderness, flavor, and color to pasta dough, and increase the protein content and elasticity of softer flours such as 00. While most recipes call for whole eggs, some can be made with only egg yolks, which provide a richer dough. Water is used more commonly with high-protein flour like durum, which produces a strong dough without the need for additional protein.

The Role of Oil and Salt

There is much debate over adding anything other than eggs, water, and flour to a dough. Oil in the dough yields a softer dough that is easier to roll out when using coarser flours.

Italians universally agree on heavily salting the cooking water for pasta, as this is the only time the pasta itself will be seasoned. This is why we also don't need to add salt to our dough, since the salted water will add flavor.

In this book, we will use as few ingredients as possible, omitting oil and salt in the dough.

The Importance of Kneading and Resting

Once you combine your flour and liquid, the next step is to knead the dough. This can be done with your hands—the Italian nonna method—or with a variety of kitchen tools, such as a food processor or stand mixer.

Kneading the dough develops the gluten, giving the dough the strength to hold its shape when it is boiled. The dough must be worked until it is springy and elastic, meaning it bounces back easily when lightly touched. Pasta dough isn't as elastic as bread dough, which is really stretchy, but holds itself together in a tight ball.

After kneading, dough should rest for at least 30 minutes. During the resting stage, the gluten in the dough relaxes, making the dough more pliable and easier to roll out, cut, and shape. Wrap the dough tightly in plastic wrap so that it does not dry out, and leave it at room temperature to rest.

All About Texture

A pasta's texture varies based on the flour used. A fresh egg dough made with very fine 00 flour and eggs is silky and rich. The dough is smooth, soft, and easy to roll out into very thin sheets to use for cut and stuffed pastas. The pasta made from this dough pairs perfectly with butter-based sauces. Dough made with coarse semolina flour and water is tougher and more difficult to roll out into sheets, so it is best suited for hand-rolled pasta shapes that require a sturdier dough. These shapes, with their rough texture, are perfect for tomato-based sauces. Whole-wheat dough, with the larger specks of bran and germ intact, has a hearty texture and nutty flavor and is especially well suited to rich meat and cheese sauces.

Key Sauce Ingredients

Canned or boxed tomatoes: Italian pantries always have a few jars of "passata," which is just tomato puree used as a base for sauces. Depending on your preference for smooth versus chunky sauces, keep crushed or diced tomatoes on hand for a quick sauce. Look at the ingredient list—the fewer ingredients, the better. Boxed brands from Italy, like Pomi, contain only tomatoes with no preservatives.

Canned fish: Oil-packed fish in tins are a pantry staple in Italy, and used to add a salty, savory bite to sauces. Look for salt-cured anchovies from Italian specialty stores if you can find them, or substitute olive oil packed–anchovies, sardines, or tuna imported from Italy or Spain.

Cheese: Always have Parmigiano-Reggiano or Pecorino Romano on hand. Grated cheeses sold in stores have fillers, so buy a solid hunk of these hard Italian cheeses and grate as needed. Parmigiano has a nuttier and milder taste, while Pecorino is saltier and more savory.

Prosciutto and pancetta: Most stores sell these cured meats diced in containers. These are essential for a quick carbonara or to add flavor to any type of pasta sauce or broth. Prosciutto has less fat than pancetta, and I use them interchangeably.

Panna or cream: Adding a little bit of light or heavy cream to sauces gives extra flavor or body. In Italy, panna is sold in boxes and kept handy to add to sauces in small doses.

Pasta water: Sometimes called "cooking water," this is the starchy water many recipes ask you to reserve (from a few tablespoons to ½ cup, depending on the recipe) when you strain the cooked pasta. It is an important final ingredient to help emulsify a sauce so it coats and clings to the pasta.

Regional Favorites

Italian food is hyper-regional, varying even between neighboring towns. Recipes reflect where the cook is from, the climate, economics, and even political history.

Northern Italy has historically been wealthy, and its pastas are indulgent, made with egg dough, stuffed with meats and cheeses, and topped with rich butter sauces and truffles. In traditionally humbler Southern Italy, pasta is made with flour and water, formed into shapes, and sauced with ragùs made with tough cuts of meat braised with tomatoes until tender enough to eat.

In both regions, recipes mainly come from what the land provides and what is in season. In Northern Italy, with its wide plains and pastures, there is plenty of beef and cow's milk for rich ingredients like Parmigiano-Reggiano and meat fillings. In mountainous and rugged Southern Italy, where only sheep can graze, the sharper sheep's milk cheese—Pecorino—is more common, along with pigs raised for cured pork products like salami and 'nduja.

This map gives you a good sense of the regions around the boot and the pasta shapes, styles, and sauces they're known for.

1. **Abruzzo**–Anellini alla Pecorara (page 98)
2. **Calabria**–Fusilli al Ferretto with 'Nduja Sauce (page 96)
3. **Campania**–Fusilli La Genovese (page 166)
4. **Emilia-Romagna**–Tagliatelle Ragù Bolognese (page 44)
5. **Lazio**–Spaghetti Carbonara (page 152)
6. **Liguria**–Trofie with Basil-Pecan Pesto (page 93)
7. **Lombardy**–Scarpinocc with Fontina in Butter Sauce (page 121)
8. **Molise**–Cavatelli with Short Rib Ragù (page 106)
9. **Piedmont**–Agnolotti del Plin (page 112)
10. **Puglia**–Orecchiette with Garlic-Broccoli Sauce (page 82)
11. **Sardinia**–Culurgiones with Tomato Sauce (page 119)
12. **Sicily**–Busiate with Pesto alla Trapanese (page 87)
13. **Tuscany**–Herbed Pappardelle with Mushroom Ragù (page 56)
14. **Trentino**–Alto Aldige—Canederli in Brodo (page 182)
15. **Veneto**–Gluten-Free Casunziei all'Ampezzana (page 138)

14. Trentino-Alto Aldige

7. Lombardy

15. Veneto

4. Emilia-Romagna

6. Liguria

9. Piedmont

13. Tuscany

1. Abruzzo

8. Molise

5. Lazio

10. Puglia

3. Campania

11. Sardinia

2. Calabria

12. Sicily

Pasta as Craft

Once you've gained a thorough understanding of the science behind pasta-making, the rest is art. With its humble beginnings in cucina povera—literally translated to "poor kitchen"—as a way to produce filling, relatively inexpensive food, pasta-making is now a treasured culinary art form. From the regional cooking of Italy to the closely guarded secrets of Italian nonnas to the hundreds of Instagram pages dedicated solely to pasta-making, there are thousands of variations. Many of these are rooted in local and family traditions, but more and more are coming from chefs and home cooks with a renewed passion for pasta-making.

With easier access to ingredients and pasta-making tools online, and the increasing prevalence of farmers' markets where you can find locally milled flours and specialty produce, home pasta-making is accessible outside of Italy more than ever before. You can be an Italian nonna–level pasta-maker with a little practice, some creativity, and a lot of flour!

Flours

Since flour is the main ingredient in pasta-making, it is important to understand how the wheat affects its texture, consistency, and the final pasta product, depending on how it is milled or where it is grown. There are two types of wheat grown in Italy: grano tenero, a soft white wheat usually grown in the North, and grano duro, a hard wheat flour from the South (though now both flours are grown all over Italy). Trying to classify all the varieties within these categories can get quite confusing, but I will try to lay it out here in the simplest way, in terms of grain type and milled size.

Double Zero or Tipo 00
With an almost powder-like consistency, this is the most finely milled flour. It has the lowest gluten content and produces a soft, tender dough. Since 00 refers to how the flour is milled and not the type of flour, this flour could be made from either grano tenero or grano duro. For our purposes, we will use only tipo 00 grano tenero for fresh pasta dough used for cut pasta, stuffed pasta, and some hand-shaped pasta. The label on the flour indicates whether it is grano tenero or grano duro. Caputo flour imported from Italy is commonly available—look for "soft wheat" on the label.

Durum Wheat
This golden-yellow grano duro has a high protein and gluten content, which results in more structure and stronger dough. Durum wheat flours are also further distinguished by the size of the grains after milling: coarse or fine.

SEMOLINA

With grains resembling sand, this is the most common version of durum wheat outside of Italy. Since the grains absorb a lot of water, the dough is firm and the pasta very chewy. It can usually be found in bulk food aisles in specialty grocery stores or from flour companies like King Arthur or Bob's Red Mill.

SEMOLA

The more finely milled version of semolina is also called "semola grano duro." In the United States, this flour is usually referred to as "durum wheat" or "fancy durum wheat." Semola is widely available in Italy and produces an easier dough to work with than coarser-grained semolina. This is why it is used among the pasta-makers of Southern Italy for hand-shaped pasta like orecchiette. Look for this online from Caputo, and make sure it says "rimacinata," which means "re-milled" and refers to the fine, powdery grind of the grain. While semola is easier to find outside of Italy now, using a blend of 50 percent semolina and 50 percent 00 or all-purpose flour will get you similar results.

All-Purpose

This is a good substitute for 00 flour and can be used to make most of the recipes in this book. With a protein content in between grano duro and grano tenero flours, it will still make perfectly fine pasta, though it won't produce a dough quite as soft and tender as 00 flour because it isn't as finely milled.

Gluten-Free

This flour is made with corn, chickpeas, rice, buckwheat, or a combination. Flours without gluten need a stabilizer in order to form a dough that will hold together for pasta. The most typical stabilizers are xanthan gum or guar gum. You can make your own gluten-free blend, but there are also plenty of gluten-free flours that already have the binder included, so all you need to do is mix the flour with eggs to make pasta dough. Cup4Cup or King Arthur Measure for Measure Flour are two brands with stabilizers that work well for pasta.

Water

Adding the right amount of water to your flour will help hydrate the grains and activate the proteins that form gluten. Water can be used in place of eggs in any dough, though it is used more commonly in pasta doughs made with durum wheat. Lukewarm water (about 100°F) is used with semolina dough to help hydrate the coarser grains, which develop the protein better and make the pasta chewier. Depending on the type of flour and how much liquid it absorbs, the water to flour ratio will vary based on a variety of factors like humidity and grain size.

Eggs

Eggs add fat and protein to pasta dough, which helps the pasta hold its shape. This is why bread bakers use more eggs in shaped breads like challah—fat affects the gluten formation to make the dough stretchier and easier to shape. As eggs are one of only two ingredients in fresh egg pasta dough, you should use the freshest, highest-quality eggs. To test the freshness of an egg, gently place it in a bowl of cold water: if it sinks to the bottom, it is fresh. Chickens that have diets heavy in green plants and corn will produce a creamy, darker yellow-orange yolk, which gives a beautiful color to fresh pasta. Try your local farmers' market for the freshest eggs.

Oil and Salt

With olive trees that are thousands of years old, Italy is a proud producer of olive oil. Choose extra-virgin for the purest and smoothest flavor. Extra-virgin oil is extracted without any added chemicals and is from the first pressing of the olives. Look for oil in green bottles or tins, since light deteriorates oils.

As mentioned earlier, most Italian cooks don't use salt in pasta dough. For sauces and boiling water, I recommend using kosher or sea salt because they have less additives than table salt.

Essential Equipment

Pasta can be made with nothing but your hands, a rolling pin, and a knife. But there are a few simple tools that will make your pasta-making easier.

For Making Pasta

Having the right tools on hand will set you up for success. This list covers the common tools you'll see mentioned frequently in this book.

Pasta board: A board measuring approximately 3 feet by 4 feet is ideal for making dough by hand, cutting pasta, and forming shapes. It is easy to scrape clean and will prevent damage to your counter when you cut pasta. Pasta boards have a lip that holds them against the table, but a large wooden cutting board would also work well.

Gnocchi board: This small, wooden paddle-shaped board has ridges on the surface to help shape gnocchi and add consistent textures, which will hold sauce.

Mattarello: A 2- to 3-foot long, thin rolling pin without handles used to roll out pasta dough. This is different from a rolling pin on a spindle with handles, which is not wide enough to roll out pasta dough.

Manual pasta machine: Included is a smooth roller to thin out the dough and two cutting rollers to cut pasta into different widths: the wide cutter is for fettuccine/tagliatelle and the narrow cutter is for spaghetti/angel hair. I recommend the type that has all three rollers on one piece rather than separate cutters that need to be attached to the back. These one-piece models are sturdier and will last longer. I prefer the Marcato Atlas brand. That said, with the right pasta attachments, a stand mixer can be used in place of the manual pasta roller. The only difference is that the rollers are powered by a motor instead of a hand crank.

Pasta extruder: Though most commonly seen in a factory, there are extruders available for home use. Several stand mixers offer attachments with metal dies that are sturdy enough to handle extruded pasta dough. Some stand-alone motorized models made by Marcato and Philips have the added benefit of making and extruding the dough all in one machine. Others use a hand-crank to feed dough through.

Pastry scraper: A flat, rectangular piece of metal or plastic used to scrape flour and cut pasta dough.

Pastry wheel: These can be used to cut long pasta or pasta shapes with fluted edges, and to cut and seal stuffed pastas. Look for one with two wheels—one smooth and one fluted, or get one of each.

Food processor: A 10- to 14-cup food processor can be used to make egg pasta dough, fillings, and sauces.

Pastry bag: Used to help pipe filling for stuffed pasta to make uniform shapes and sizes.

Potato ricer: This is used to finely mill potatoes through a plate of small holes, which is the first step to making fluffy potato gnocchi.

Ravioli mold: A tray and press for making multiple uniform ravioli at one time. I recommend a mold with holes for each ravioli, which makes it less likely the dough will stick.

Ravioli stamps: Metal stamps in various shapes and sizes used to seal and cut ravioli.

For Drying and Storing

All pasta can be dried or frozen for later use. You can twirl long pasta into loose nests to dry out for a day, then store them in your pantry. Pasta can be stored frozen or dried in an airtight storage container for two to three months.

Sheet pan: Have a few of these on hand for laying out pasta to dry or freeze.

Drying rack: A pasta drying rack is used to hang long, cut pasta to dry.

For Cooking and Serving

You'll need large pots to give your pasta plenty of room to cook, along with large sauté pans to make sauce and marry it to the pasta.

Pasta should always be cooked in heavily salted water, since this is the only time the pasta itself is seasoned. Use 4 quarts of water for a pound of pasta, and add 1 to 2 tablespoons of salt or a healthy handful of salt if you want to use the nonna method and not measure.

The heavily salted water becomes starchy when cooking the pasta. As you will see later, you may need this pasta water for the sauce. Do not plop sauce on top of strained pasta. Pasta should always be married to the sauce, meaning you should always add the pasta to a pan of simmering sauce or add sauce ingredients to cook with the pasta. The best setup for cooking and saucing pasta is to have your pasta stockpot on the stovetop next to the pan you are simmering your sauce in so you can combine the pasta and sauce to finish cooking together.

Large stockpot: Pot size should be at least 6 quarts so you can fill it about two-thirds with water for a pound of pasta.

Large sauté pan: A 4- to 5-quart pan is ideal for cooking all types of sauces and has enough room to add your pasta to the sauce to cook together so the pasta is coated properly.

Pasta fork, tongs, or spider: Use tongs or a pasta fork to pull out long pastas and put them directly into the sauté pan with the sauce. Use a pasta spider, a wide shallow skimmer with a long handle, to pull pasta shapes out of the water.

Upgrades

You may find that as pasta-making becomes a regular pursuit, other more specialized pieces of equipment find their way onto your wish list. None are absolute musts for the recipes in this book, but they may be worth looking into as you level up your handmade pasta-making.

Corzetti stamp: Corzetti pasta from Liguria resembles coins with a stamped image. There are custom-made stamps available that can be engraved with names, family seals, or any image you might like from artisan woodworkers.

Bigoli press: Also called a "torchio," this is one of the oldest types of pasta-makers. Pasta dough is placed in a long tube and a screw is turned to push the pasta through a die to make bigoli—a long, thick, hollow pasta similar to bucatini.

Cavatelli maker: A small hand-crank machine that attaches to a table. A strip of dough is pushed through a small ridged roller to produce cavatelli.

Bicicletta (pasta bike): An adjustable pasta cutter with interchangeable wheels that can be adjusted to cut uniform strips or squares of pasta.

CHAPTER 2
Mastering the Dough

It's helpful to have a step-by-step guide when you begin pasta-making, from combining the raw ingredients to proper kneading. In this chapter, we'll focus mostly on the handmade method but also touch on how you can use a stand mixer or food processor to make dough. After covering all the steps to get your pasta dough to the resting stage, I will show you how to roll it out using a pasta machine and then review the nonna method using a rolling pin. Of course, sometimes the dough doesn't cooperate, but there are plenty of tips on how to troubleshoot, and also some key advice for storing your pasta creations.

MAKE A WELL

BEAT EGGS TO MIX

SCRAPE TO MIX

STRETCH AND KNEAD

FOLD AND KNEAD

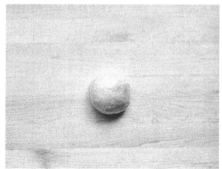

LET REST

Mixing by Hand

Making dough by hand is the best way to learn how to get the right texture for pasta. You will feel the flour and water transform in your hands from a messy pile to a firm ball of dough ready to be turned into pasta. Even when using a mixer to make dough, it is always best to finish kneading it by hand to make sure it is the right consistency. Here's how to do it, from top to bottom. This method uses my Egg Pasta Dough (page 32), but these skills apply to any dough recipe in the book.

Step One: Prep

1. About half an hour before making dough, remove the eggs from the refrigerator so they come to room temperature. Room-temperature eggs bind more easily to the flour.

2. A hard wood surface like a pasta board (see page 12) is best for making, cutting, and shaping pasta dough. Avoid making dough on stainless steel or granite counters because the dough needs a little warmth to develop properly.

3. Bring out your kitchen scale or measuring cups. It is best to weigh flour with a scale for dough recipes, but since most nonnas do it by feel, measuring cups will work as well.

4. Have a rubber or metal pastry scraper, some plastic wrap, and a dinner fork at the ready.

Step Two: Make a Well

1. Measure or weigh the flour.

2. Pour the flour into a mound on the pasta board.

3. Using your fingers, push the flour out of the center of the mound to make a wide, shallow well that has walls of equal width all around. You are working to create a ring of flour with a bare center that goes all the way down to the wood to make a barrier to hold the eggs. Make sure it's wide enough: if it's too small, the eggs will overflow.

4. Add your eggs to the center of the well. Alternatively, you can whisk the eggs in a bowl first and then pour them into the well.

5. Add to the well any other ingredients a dough recipe calls for: herbs, vegetables, or spices to flavor the dough.

Machine Mixing

If you are making a lot of dough for your pantry or having a big dinner party, using a machine is faster and easier on your hands. You can use either a food processor (only for soft wheat doughs) or a stand mixer. Once the dough is mixed, dump it out onto a board and knead for 1 to 2 minutes by hand to form it into a tight ball. Check the dough by pressing it with your finger. If it bounces back, it is done.

Food Processor

1. Use the chopping blade on a 14-cup food processor.
2. Add the flour and pulse a few times to aerate. Add any flavorings a recipe calls for. Pulse a few times to chop up and distribute them.
3. Crack the eggs into a small bowl.
4. Turn on the food processor and slowly pour the eggs through the spout.
5. Run the processor until a dough ball forms. The inside of the bowl should be clean at this point, as the ball rotates around the blade and the side of the bowl. If the dough is sticking to the sides of the bowl, add more flour 1 tablespoon at a time. If the dough is crumbly and won't form into a ball, add water 1 tablespoon at a time until it comes together.
6. Let the machine run 2 to 3 minutes. The dough ball will spin around the bowl, which will knead the dough.

   Note: Do not leave the food processor unattended while mixing the dough.

Stand Mixer

1. Set up the stand mixer with the flat beater attachment.
2. Add the flour and eggs to the bowl.
3. Run the mixer on the second-lowest speed until the eggs are broken up and the flour is incorporated into the liquid.
4. Remove the beater and replace it with the dough hook, scraping off any dough from the beater first.
5. Run on the second-lowest speed for 5 minutes. If the dough is sticky, add more flour 1 tablespoon at a time. If the dough is crumbly and won't form into a ball, add water 1 tablespoon at a time until it comes together.

Step Three: Mix

1. Using a fork, gently beat the eggs in the center of the well until the yolks and whites are thoroughly blended, being careful not to overflow the walls of the well.

2. Use the fork to pull some of the flour from the inside of the well into the egg mixture. Mix until the flour is absorbed by the eggs. Repeat, gradually adding flour and beating the egg until the mixture begins to look shaggy.

3. Scrape the remaining dough off the fork into the mixture. Use the pastry scraper to combine the rest of the flour. Slide the scraper under the shaggy pile of flour, and fold the mixture over multiple times, until the flour and eggs come together into a solid lump. The dough will be dry at this point.

4. Gather all the dough into a ball with your hands and set aside. Then use the pastry scraper to scrape the pasta board clean of dried dough.

Step Four: Knead

1. Using the heel of your hand and firm pressure, push the dough down and away from you at the same time, being careful not to smash the dough straight down into the board. You are stretching the dough, not trying to flatten it.

2. If the dough sticks to your hand or the board, add a tablespoon at a time of flour to be incorporated as you knead.

3. Rotate the dough a quarter turn, fold in half, and repeat, pushing the dough firmly down and away.

4. Continue kneading in this manner until the dough starts to look smooth and becomes elastic. This should take 5 to 10 minutes; any longer and the dough may dry out.

5. Test the dough by gently pressing on it with your finger. When it springs back easily, it means the dough is ready to rest. If the dough is still too soft and doesn't spring back, continue to knead and test until it does.

Step Five: Let Rest

1. Wrap the dough tightly in plastic, making sure to remove all the air so that it doesn't dry out.

2. Rest the dough for approximately 30 minutes to an hour (do not refrigerate). During this time, the gluten that was formed during the kneading will begin to relax, which will make it easier to roll out the dough into sheets or shapes. The dough will lose some springiness as it rests.

3. While pasta dough is best used right away, if you would like to use the dough later, you can refrigerate it for up to 3 days or freeze it for later use. To freeze, tightly wrap the dough in plastic wrap to remove as much air as possible. When ready to use, leave the dough out for 2 to 3 hours until it comes back to room temperature.

Rolling Out Dough with a Machine

Now that you have a rested and pliable pasta dough, it's time to roll it out to form it into cut and shaped pasta. Use a tabletop pasta machine with a handle to manually turn the rollers to thin out the dough. If you're using a stand mixer's pasta attachment or a machine with a motor instead, the only difference is that you have an extra hand to work with, since you do not need to use the handle to turn the rollers.

1. Attach the pasta machine to a table or countertop. Pull out the adjustment knob on the side to set the roller to the widest setting (usually 1 or 0).

2. Remove one-quarter of the rested dough from the plastic, and rewrap the remaining dough.

3. Use your hands to form the dough into a rectangle about the size of a deck of cards and ¼ inch thick.

4. Use the machine to knead the dough to reactivate the gluten by feeding it through the widest roller setting a few times. This needs to be done before the dough can be thinned out. Start by feeding the dough through the roller, then fold the dough in half and repeat three or four times until the dough is strong and can be stretched without tearing. The dough should feel slightly tacky, like a wrung-out dish towel. If the dough is sticky or wet, lay it on the pasta board and rub flour on each side.

5. Begin to thin out the dough by adjusting the rollers on the pasta machine and turning the dial up one level each time you feed the dough through the rollers. You may need to flour the sheet lightly between steps if it starts to stick. I recommend

stopping at the setting numbered 7 or 8 for cut pasta and 6 for stuffed pasta—or until you can just start to see your fingers through the dough.

6. Now your sheet is ready to be transformed into pasta! Repeat with the remaining dough, rewrapping the unused portion each time.

. . . Or a Rolling Pin

You can use the nonna method to roll out dough with a mattarello—the long, thin Italian rolling pin designed for pasta-making (see page 13). A wooden rolling pin gives the dough a rougher texture than a machine with stainless steel rollers. Some people prefer this texture because the pasta holds the sauce better.

1. Lightly flour your pasta board.

2. Remove the dough from the plastic wrap and use your hands to flatten the dough ball into a disk.

3. Roll the dough with the pin by pushing it away from you. Turn the dough a quarter turn and continue rolling and turning until it begins to thin out. If the dough sticks to the board or the pin, rub some flour on top of the dough and continue to roll.

4. Stretch the dough by wrapping three-quarters of it around the pin and letting the remaining one-quarter hang off the pasta board. Stretch the dough by pushing the wrapped pin away from you, making sure the hanging flap stays in place. Unfurl the dough from the pin and repeat, giving the dough a quarter turn each time.

5. Lay out the pasta sheet. Roll the dough away from you, then rotate a quarter turn and repeat three times.

6. Repeat steps 4 and 5 until the dough is thin enough so you can just see your hand through the sheet of dough, or approximately 1/16 inch.

Dough FAQs

Are you running into problems while making pasta? Here are some suggestions on how to troubleshoot.

Q: Why does my pasta dough stick to itself when it comes out of the pasta roller?

A: The dough is too wet. As you thin it out, you are squeezing out some of the extra liquid, which is why it gets wetter as you go and requires more flour. The dough should be tacky, but not wet or sticky. To fix this, lay your pasta sheet down on the pasta board and lightly flour each side of the dough. Rub the flour across the entire sheet with your hands so the flour is evenly distributed, instead of just sprinkling it on top. Continue to thin the dough, adding flour to the sheet only if it is sticking, not each time you run it through the rollers.

Q: Why is my pasta dough too tough or dry?

A: This could be one of several things. You may have added too much flour while thinning. You only need to add flour when the dough starts to stick to your hands or the roller. Dry dough is also caused by exposing the dough to air—always keep your dough wrapped tightly in plastic wrap when not using. If your dough is too dry, add a little more liquid by wetting your hands and kneading the dough. Repeat this until more liquid is absorbed by the dough and the dough is more pliable. If your dough seems too tough, it needs to rest again. Wrap it in plastic and let it rest 30 minutes to an hour to help relax the gluten.

Q: My pasta turned out gummy. What should I do differently next time?

A: You may not have kneaded the dough enough. A weak dough is gummy because the gluten hasn't developed enough to add springiness. You can test this by trying to pull apart the dough with your hands. If it comes apart easily, then you should spend more time kneading it. Once you try to tear the dough apart and it resists enough to stay together, it has been kneaded enough. This is a technique I show in my classes to illustrate that kneading dough makes it stronger as you go. Try this the first few times you make pasta to see how the dough develops as you go along.

Q: Can the weather affect the dough?

A: Yes. A more humid day or climate will result in a wetter dough, so you may need to add more flour to balance out this effect. Pasta-making is sometimes more art than science, and the more you practice, the more you will get a feel for how the dough will behave under different conditions. On a humid or rainy day, I would recommend starting with a few tablespoons or grams less flour, since it will be easier to add more flour to fix a wet dough than to try to rehydrate a dry dough.

Q: My well broke and eggs are flowing out of the flour! What do I do?

A: Grab your pastry scraper to stop the flow, then throw some of the well flour on top to absorb the liquid until it is no longer runny and scrape everything back into the center of the flour. If you prefer, you can make an inverted well in a bowl to avoid this problem. Add flour to a bowl and push the flour up the sides so the bottom of the bowl is free of flour, and then add the eggs and mix the eggs and flour like you would in a well on a board. Once the dough comes together, turn it out on the pasta board to knead.

Storage

If you aren't an Italian nonna who can make pasta daily, you can make large batches and store them for later mealtime cooking. Here are some best practices.

Drying

When drying pasta, there may be some concerns about food safety for egg pasta. Cut pasta like fettuccine is thin, so it will dry quickly, removing the danger of bacteria forming. Thicker pasta like hand-shaped pici will dry more slowly, leaving too much moisture and allowing bacteria to grow. It is not recommended to dry thick or stuffed pastas. For thin extruded, shaped, or cut pasta, store in an airtight container and it will remain safe to eat for a month. For dried pasta made with eggs, you'll also want to only store them for up to a month, since eggs have fat in them and the quality will diminish over time. Pasta without eggs can be stored longer, up to 3 months.

1. Lay the pasta flat in a single layer on a sheet pan covered with parchment, or go traditional and lay it on a table covered with a tablecloth. You can also fold the pasta over or twist the pasta in loose nests to dry to make it easier to store.

2. Let the pasta dry uncovered 12 to 24 hours (a longer time is required in humid areas), turning it over halfway through so that all sides are exposed to the air.

3. Store the pasta in an airtight container 4 to 6 weeks.

Freezing

All pasta can be safely frozen and will last longer than dried pasta. Freezing works best for stuffed pastas to keep the filling fresh, but can be used for all types of pasta. To cook frozen pasta, you do not need to thaw it, but should adjust cooking time by adding an extra minute or two.

1. Lay the pasta flat in a single layer on a sheet pan covered with parchment.

2. Place the sheet pan in the freezer 24 hours.

3. Remove the pasta and store it in resealable plastic bags, removing as much air as possible.

4. Frozen pasta will last up to 6 months.

About the Recipes

We have a delicious menu of pasta recipes in this book, including traditional and treasured regional pasta recipes from all over Italy. With the resurgence of interest in pasta-making, recipes and shapes that were close to being lost are making a comeback. You will learn a number of different dough recipes to be used for specific pastas. Each recipe is accompanied by a sauce, although you can mix and match throughout the book. But first, a few tips:

1. When kneading, thinning, cutting, and shaping dough, keep an extra cup of flour (the same one the dough's recipe is based on) on hand for dusting the work surface and the pasta so it doesn't stick together.

2. You can use almost any dough recipe interchangeably, especially those made with gluten-free dough. Keep in mind that egg doughs are best for stuffed pasta and durum wheat doughs are best for shaped pasta, but gluten-free dough will work in place of these doughs, too.

3. It's preferable to use a pastry bag or resealable plastic bag with a snipped end to fill most stuffed pasta, but you can also use a spoon.

4. Pasta cooking water is an important ingredient for finishing and emulsifying most sauces, so don't forget to save some for the recipes when indicated in the method.

5. Unless given a specific amount in the ingredients list, salt and pepper should be used to season to your own preference—whether that's a light touch or several grinds. I'll note when and where to season based on a quick taste of, say, a simmering sauce. But for any cooking meats or raw ingredients, it's best to go light at first and then revisit the seasoning after the ingredients are cooked through.

6. As a finishing touch, add a few tablespoons of grated Parmesan or Pecorino to top your pasta. Or leave a small bowl of cheese on the table so you and your loved ones can sprinkle on as much as each person prefers. I favor Pecorino because it has a more savory flavor, but I tend to match the cheese to a pasta's origin on the boot: Northern Italy (Parmesan) or Southern Italy (Pecorino).

Tie on your aprons and let's get started!

Master Dough Recipes

You will learn seven master dough recipes, ranging from traditional Egg Pasta Dough (page 32) to Gluten-Free Pasta Dough (page 35). These recipes will serve as the basis for all the pasta recipes in the book, except for gnocchi (don't worry, we have a gnocchi chapter, too!). Each dough will be accompanied by a list of recommended recipes that work best with it.

We will start with Egg Pasta Dough (page 32), which is used to make cut and stuffed pasta like tagliatelle and tortellini. The pastas of Southern Italy are made with durum wheat flour—either fine semola or coarse semolina. You will learn these doughs and how to make hand-shaped pastas like orecchiette as well as extruded pasta like rigatoni. We will also make a gluten-free dough, which requires a little more technique to master but is appreciated by those who can't tolerate wheat and still want pasta. There will also be some flavored dough recipes. And to simplify pasta-making, if you cannot find the pasta flours needed for the other recipes, I will show you a simple dough made from all-purpose flour and water that can be used for most pasta recipes.

Techniques and Full Recipes

This book will take you through the process of turning dough into shapes and pasta variations. "Learn and Make" recipes are in-depth tutorials that include photos to better demonstrate the basic technique used across many recipes. Throughout, you'll learn how to create cut pasta (tagliatelle, pappardelle, and capellini); hand-shaped pasta (cavatelli, pici, and lorighittas); stuffed pasta (tortellini, ravioli, and agnolotti); extruded pasta (bucatini, rigatoni, and bigoli); and gnocchi (including gnudi and malloreddus).

Extra Sauces and Fillings

At the end of the book, there is a chapter dedicated to additional sauces and fillings that can be mixed and matched with most of the pasta recipes. Each sauce recipe will include a list of the pasta shapes with which it works best or would traditionally be served with to take out the guesswork. Certain sauces work better with specific pasta shapes and textures, but this is where your creativity can shine and you can choose your own combinations. The extra fillings are some of my favorites.

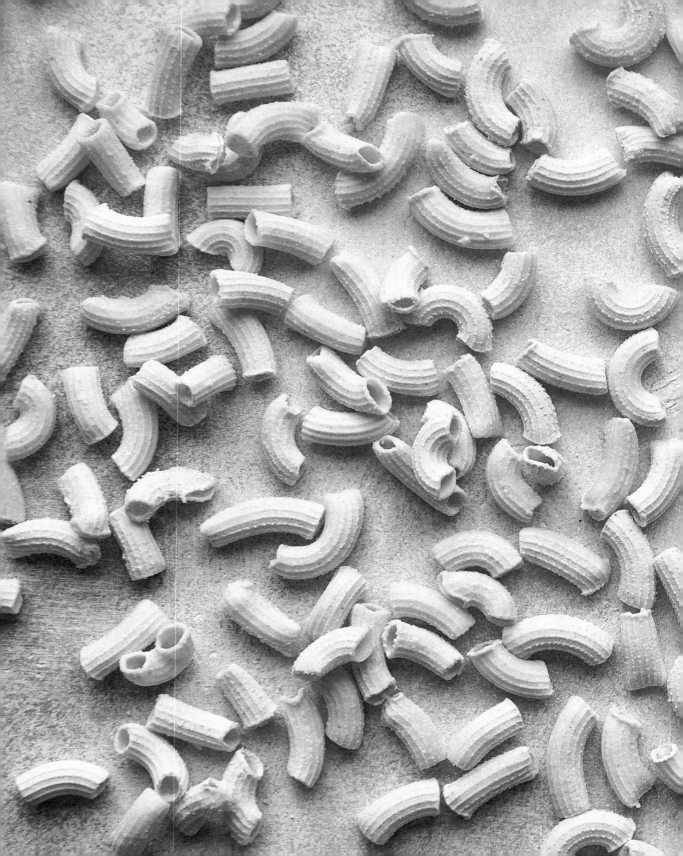

PART II

The Recipes

We've reached the fun part: the recipes! There are 100 recipes in this book, covering a wide variety of pasta and ways to serve it. Some recipes are very traditional, from specific regions of Italy, and some have been adapted to more modern tastes. First, you'll learn the master dough recipes and get a sense of which pasta shapes work best with each. Next, the pasta recipe chapters are each devoted to a different shaping technique (cut, hand-shaped, stuffed, and extruded). A chapter on gnocchi includes the recipe for their particular dough. Finally, we end with a chapter of additional sauces and fillings that can be used with different recipes throughout the book.

CHAPTER 3

Master Dough Recipes

Egg Pasta Dough

MAKES 1 POUND | PREP 20 MIN | REST 30 MIN

This is the traditional pasta dough made with eggs, which lend a rich, silky texture to pasta. This dough is perfect for long-cut pastas like fettuccine and pappardelle and holds up well for stuffed pastas like tortellini and ravioli.

TOOLS
Scale or measuring cup
Pasta board
Fork
Pastry scraper
Plastic wrap

INGREDIENTS

2 cups (300 g) 00 flour

3 large eggs

1 large egg yolk

1. **PREP.** Weigh or measure the flour onto the pasta board.

2. **MAKE A WELL.** Make a wide, shallow well in the center of the flour and add the eggs.

3. **MIX.** Beat the eggs and yolk in the center of the well until the yolks and whites are combined. Using the fork, scrape some of the flour from the inside edges of the well into the egg mixture and beat until the flour is absorbed into the egg. Repeat this step, gradually adding flour and beating until the egg mixture is no longer runny and begins to look shaggy. Use the pastry scraper to fold the rest of the flour over into the dough until it is incorporated. Gather all the dough into a ball with your hands, set it aside, and then use the pastry scraper to scrape the pasta board clean of dried dough.

4. **KNEAD.** Knead 5 to 10 minutes, until the dough bounces back when pressed lightly with your finger. Add flour one tablespoon at a time if the dough is sticky.

5. **REST.** Wrap the dough in plastic and rest at room temperature 30 minutes or in the fridge overnight. Bring back to room temperature to roll out.

TRY IT WITH: Tagliatelle Ragù Bolognese (page 44), Trenette al Pesto (page 66), Corzetti with Marjoram-Walnut Pesto (page 94), and Tortellini with Burro e Oro (page 136).

All-Purpose Flour Pasta Dough

MAKES 1 POUND | PREP 20 MIN | REST 30 MIN

This dough will work great for most pastas if you do not have access to other flours. Use water for the liquid in hand-shaped and cut pasta. For stuffed pasta, I'd recommend using eggs because it will make a stronger dough to stand up to the fillings.

INGREDIENTS

2 cups (300 g) all-purpose flour, unbleached

½ cup (130 g) warm water or 3 large eggs

TOOLS

Scale or measuring cup

Pasta board

Fork

Pastry scraper

Plastic wrap

1. **PREP.** Weigh or measure the flour onto the pasta board.

2. **MAKE A WELL.** Make a wide, shallow well in the center of the flour. Pour a few tablespoons of water into the center of the well.

3. **MIX.** Using the fork, scrape some of the flour from the inside edges of the well into the water and stir it in to make a slurry. Repeat this step, gradually adding flour and mixing until it begins to look shaggy. Use the pastry scraper to fold the rest of the flour over into the dough until it is incorporated. Gather all the dough into a ball with your hands, set aside, then use the pastry scraper to scrape the pasta board clean of dried dough.

4. **KNEAD.** Knead 8 to 10 minutes, until the dough bounces back when pressed lightly with your finger. Add flour one tablespoon at a time if dough is sticky.

5. **REST.** Wrap the dough in plastic and rest at room temperature 30 minutes or in the fridge overnight. Bring back to room temperature to roll out.

TRY IT WITH: Reginette with Asparagus Cream (page 70), Sausage Lasagna (page 74), Strozzapreti with Sausage and Broccoli Cream (page 84), and Trofie with Basil-Pecan Pesto (page 93).

Whole-Wheat Flour Pasta Dough

MAKES 1 POUND | PREP 20 MIN | REST 30 MIN

Whole-wheat flour's higher protein content makes it tough, so some people prefer a half-and-half blend of all-purpose and whole-wheat flour to soften it up. The recipe below is for an all whole-wheat flour dough, which will produce a deep brown pasta that is perfect for hearty pasta dishes with meat or cheese sauces.

TOOLS
Scale or measuring cup

Pasta board

Fork

Pastry scraper

Plastic wrap

INGREDIENTS

2 cups (300 g) whole-wheat flour
4 large eggs

1. **PREP.** Weigh or measure the flour onto the pasta board.

2. **MAKE A WELL.** Make a wide, shallow well in the center of the flour and add the eggs.

3. **MIX.** Beat the eggs in the center of the well until the yolks and whites are combined. Using the fork, scrape some of the flour from the inside edges of the well into the egg mixture and beat until the flour is absorbed into the egg. Repeat this step, gradually adding flour and beating until the egg mixture is no longer runny and begins to look shaggy. Use the pastry scraper to fold the rest of the flour over into the dough until it is incorporated. Gather all the dough into a ball with your hands, set aside, then use the pastry scraper to scrape the pasta board clean of dried dough.

4. **KNEAD.** Knead 8 to 10 minutes, until the dough bounces back when pressed lightly with your finger. Add flour one tablespoon at a time if dough is sticky.

5. **REST.** Wrap the dough in plastic and rest at room temperature 30 minutes or in the fridge overnight. Bring back to room temperature to roll out.

TRY IT WITH: Whole-Wheat Fettuccine Boscaiola (page 48), Whole-Wheat Pizzoccheri Valtellina (page 72), Whole-Wheat Pansotti with Walnut Sauce (page 126), and Whole-Wheat Bigoli Cacio e Pepe (page 160).

Gluten-Free Pasta Dough

MAKES 1 POUND | PREP 20 MIN

Gluten-free pasta requires more eggs to add protein and bind the dough. Xanthan gum makes the dough elastic in place of gluten. Some gluten-free flours include a binder, such as Cup4Cup: if you're using these, omit the xanthan gum. The dough requires that you make your well inside of a bowl, and you won't need to do as much kneading as there is no gluten to activate.

INGREDIENTS

2 cups (300 g) gluten-free flour

1 tablespoon (13 g) xanthan gum

3 large egg yolks
3 whole large eggs

TOOLS
Scale or measuring cup
Mixing bowl
Fork
Pasta board
Plastic wrap

1. **PREP.** Weigh or measure the flour and xanthan gum into a mixing bowl and stir together.

2. **MAKE A WELL.** Make a well of flour inside the bowl by pushing the flour up the side of the bowl. Add the eggs and yolks to the center of the bowl.

3. **MIX.** Beat the eggs in the center of the well, until the yolks and whites are combined. Using the fork, scrape some of the flour from the outside edges of the well into the egg mixture and beat until the flour is absorbed into the egg. Repeat this step, gradually adding flour and stirring until all the flour is incorporated.

4. **KNEAD.** Gather all the dough into a ball with your hands and place on a well-floured pasta board. Knead 4 to 5 minutes, until smooth.

5. **REST.** Technically, gluten-free dough doesn't need to rest and can be used right away. It should, however, be wrapped tightly in plastic so it doesn't dry out. Slice the dough into ¼-inch flat pieces to roll out.

TRY IT WITH: Gluten-Free Capellini with Lemon-Garlic Shrimp (page 68), Gluten-Free Anolini in Brodo (page 122), Gluten-Free Cannelloni Lucchese (page 124), and Gluten-Free Casunziei all'Ampezzana (page 138).

Semolina Pasta Dough

MAKES 1 POUND | PREP 20 MIN | REST 30 MIN

Coarse semolina flour was traditionally reserved for factory-made pasta, but new tools allow you to make shapes like spaghetti or rigatoni at home. The dough recipe below is for extruded pasta only and must be mixed in a stand mixer, since it's dry and doesn't form a ball. If using for handmade pasta, use a 2:1 ratio of semolina to warm water and follow the instructions for Semola Rimacinata Pasta Dough (page 37).

TOOLS
Scale or measuring cup
Stand mixer with paddle
Plastic wrap

INGREDIENTS

2 cups (300 g) semolina flour
⅓ cup (80 g) lukewarm water

1. **PREP.** Weigh or measure the flour into the bowl of a stand mixer.

2. **MIX.** Pour in a few tablespoons of water and run the mixer on speed 4 for 1 minute, until the liquid is absorbed by the flour. Add the rest of the water and run on speed 4 for 5 minutes. The dough will look like loose pebbles and will just hold together in a loose ball when squeezed.

3. **REST.** Cover the mixing bowl with plastic wrap until ready to extrude the pasta.

TRY IT WITH: Bucatini all'Amatriciana (page 158), Spaghetti Carbonara (page 152), and Macaroni with Sausage and Peppers (page 164).

Semola Rimacinata Pasta Dough

MAKES 1 POUND | PREP 20 MIN | REST 30 MIN

Finely milled semola rimacinata flour is commonly used in Southern Italian handmade pasta. It works best for handmade shapes like orecchiette because the tough dough holds its shape well. Kneading semola is a workout—this dough fights back! If you can't find semola, use a half-and-half mix of semolina and tipo 00 or all-purpose flour.

INGREDIENTS

2 cups (300 g) semola flour
⅔ cup (160 g) lukewarm water

TOOLS
Scale or measuring cup
Pasta board
Fork
Pastry scraper
Plastic wrap

1. **PREP.** Weigh or measure the flour onto the pasta board.

2. **MAKE A WELL.** Make a wide, shallow well in the center of the flour. Pour a few tablespoons of water into the center of the well.

3. **MIX.** Using the fork, scrape some of the flour from the inside edges of the well into the water and stir until absorbed into a paste. Repeat this step with a few more tablespoons of water at a time to slowly hydrate the flour. Once all the water is added, use the pastry scraper to fold the rest of the flour over into the dough until it is incorporated. Gather all the dough into a ball with your hands, set aside, then use the pastry scraper to scrape the pasta board clean of dried dough.

4. **KNEAD.** Knead with a firm pressure for 8 to 10 minutes until the dough bounces back when pressed lightly with your finger. Add flour one tablespoon at a time if dough is sticky.

5. **REST.** Wrap the dough in plastic and rest at room temperature 30 minutes or in the fridge overnight. Bring back to room temperature to roll out.

TRY IT WITH: Lagane and Ceci (page 53), Busiate with Pesto alla Trapanese (page 87), Fusilli al Ferretto with 'Nduja Sauce (page 96), and Cavatelli with Short Rib Ragù (page 106).

Flavored Pasta Dough

MAKES 1 POUND | PREP 20 MIN | REST 30 MIN

You can add a variety of ingredients, like herbs, pureed vegetables, or spices, to pasta dough to create beautiful colors and flavors. This recipe uses spinach, but you can experiment with the other variations listed here, too. Adding ingredients with a high water content like spinach will make the dough wetter, so add a few extra tablespoons of flour as needed.

TOOLS

Scale or measuring cup

Pasta board

Fork

Pastry scraper

Plastic wrap

INGREDIENTS

2 cups (300 g) 00 flour

3 large eggs
1 large egg yolk

1 cup minced fresh spinach leaves (or other flavor option*)

*flavor options

1 cup minced kale leaves

½ cup red beet puree

½ cup tomato paste

2 teaspoons black pepper

1 tablespoon chili powder

½ cup minced fresh basil or other herbs

2 tablespoons garlic powder

1. **PREP.** Weigh or measure the flour onto the pasta board.

2. **MAKE A WELL.** Make a wide, shallow well in the center of the flour and add the eggs, yolk, and spinach (or other ingredient from the flavor options list).

3. **MIX.** Beat the eggs in the center of the well until the yolks and whites are combined. Using the fork, scrape some of the flour from the inside edges of the well into the egg mixture and beat until the flour is absorbed into the egg. Repeat this step, gradually adding flour and beating until the egg mixture is no longer runny and begins to look shaggy. Use the pastry scraper to fold the rest of the flour over into the dough until it is incorporated. Gather all the dough into a ball with your hands, set aside, then use the pastry scraper to scrape the pasta board clean of dried dough.

4. **KNEAD.** Knead 5 to 10 minutes, until the dough bounces back when pressed lightly with your finger. Add flour one tablespoon at a time if dough is sticky.

5. **REST.** Wrap the dough in plastic and rest at room temperature 30 minutes or in the fridge overnight. Bring back to room temperature to roll out.

TRY IT WITH: Herbed Pappardelle with Mushroom Ragù (page 56), Spinach Garganelli with Prosciutto (page 88), Basil Farfalle with Ricotta and Cherry Tomatoes (page 90), and Corn and Mascarpone Mezzaluna with Basil Oil (page 142).

CHAPTER 4

Cut Pasta

Gluten-Free Capellini with Lemon-Garlic Shrimp, page 68

Tagliatelle

SERVES 4 | PREP 20 MIN

Tagliatelle is the classic cut of pasta from Bologna, traditionally served with a rich meat ragù. There is a "golden tagliatelle" registered with Bologna's chamber of commerce, which specifies the exact width: 7 millimeters. Just keep yours between ¼ and ⅓ inch.

TOOLS

Tools for Egg Pasta Dough (page 32)

Pasta machine

INGREDIENTS

1 Egg Pasta Dough recipe (page 32)

1. **MAKE THE DOUGH.** Make the Egg Pasta Dough.

2. **KNEAD.** Attach the pasta machine to a table or countertop. Pull the knob on the side and turn to adjust the roller to the widest setting. Divide the dough into quarters, and wrap three of the pieces in plastic so you can work in batches. Form one of the dough quarters into a rectangle about the size of a deck of cards, ¼ inch thick. Use the machine to knead the dough to reactivate the gluten by feeding it through the widest roller setting. Fold the dough in half and repeat three to four times until the dough is strong and can be stretched without tearing. The dough should feel slightly tacky, like a wrung-out dish towel. If it's sticky or wet, lay the sheet on the pasta board and rub a little flour on each side.

3. **THIN.** Begin to thin out the dough by adjusting the rollers on the pasta machine, turning the dial up by one number each time you feed it through the rollers. You may need to flour the sheet between steps if it starts to stick. Tagliatelle should be thin, so roll out the dough until you can see your fingers through the sheet. Lay the finished sheet flat on the pasta board and liberally flour on both sides so it doesn't stick when cut.

4. **CUT.** Switch the handle to the widest cutting roller. Center the pasta sheet, and roll the pasta through the cutters, catching the strands as they come out on the other side. Alternatively, roll up the floured sheet jelly-roll style, and use a knife to cut the pasta into ¼-inch-wide strips. Unroll the tagliatelle.

5. **FLOUR.** Flour the tagliatelle liberally, and then twirl into loose nests or lay flat until ready to use.

KNEAD

FOLD

THIN

FLOUR SHEETS

CUT

FLOUR AND TWIRL

TIP: As you thin out your pasta sheet, make sure to flour it as soon as you notice it sticking, or else it will get jammed up in the roller.

Tagliatelle Ragù Bolognese

SERVES 4 | PREP 30 MIN | COOK 2 TO 3 HRS

A meaty, wine-scented sauce is the classic pairing for tagliatelle. Note that traditionally this is a meat-based sauce flecked with some tomatoes, not a tomato-based sauce with meat, as "Bolognese" has come to mean outside of Bologna.

TOOLS

Tools for Egg Pasta Dough (page 32)

Pasta machine

Knife

Large stockpot

FOR THE TAGLIATELLE

1 Egg Pasta Dough recipe (page 32)

1. **MAKE THE DOUGH.** Make the Egg Pasta Dough.

2. **THIN AND CUT.** Thin the pasta sheets until you can just see your fingers through them. Rub flour liberally on each side of the sheets. Using the wide cutter on the pasta machine, run the sheets through to cut, or use a knife to cut into ¼-inch strips.

FOR THE SAUCE

2 tablespoons olive oil
½ cup minced onion
½ cup minced carrot
½ cup minced celery
1 pound ground pork

1 pound ground beef
Salt and pepper
½ bottle of red wine

2 cups crushed tomatoes or tomato sauce
¼ cup heavy cream

1. **COOK.** Coat the bottom of a large pot with the oil, add the onion, carrot, and celery, and sauté on low to medium heat until soft, 8 minutes. Add the pork and beef, season with salt and pepper, and cook until the meat is browned, 8 to 10 minutes. Add the red wine, turn the heat to medium-high, and let simmer 8 to 10 minutes or until the wine is cooked off.

2. **SIMMER.** Add the tomatoes or sauce and let simmer, covered, 2 to 3 hours, stirring occasionally.

3. **BOIL.** Bring a large pot of salted water to a boil. Add the pasta, stir, and cook 1 to 2 minutes. Strain.

4. **SAUCE.** Turn off the heat, add the cream, and stir it into the sauce. Add the tagliatelle and stir until coated.

> **TIP:** Use lean ground beef to minimize the amount of oil. The pork adds the fat missing from leaner beef. If you use meat with a higher fat content, you may need to skim off some of the oil prior to adding cream.

Capellini with Fresh Tomato Sauce

SERVES 4 | PREP 30 MIN

Capellini, or angel hair, is the thinnest long-cut pasta. It pairs perfectly with light, fresh sauces. It cooks very quickly, especially when made with fresh egg dough. This sauce, served at room temperature, is perfect for a summer day when you do not want to have a lot of pots cooking.

TOOLS

Tools for Egg
Pasta Dough
(page 32)

Pasta
machine

Knife

Food
processor
or blender

Large
serving bowl

Large
stockpot

FOR THE CAPELLINI

1 Egg Pasta Dough recipe (page 32)

1. **MAKE THE DOUGH.** Make the Egg Pasta Dough.

2. **THIN AND CUT.** Thin the pasta sheets until you can just see your fingers through them. Rub flour liberally on each side of the sheets. Using the narrow cutter on the pasta machine, run the sheets through to cut, or use a knife to cut into strips less than ⅛ inch wide.

FOR THE SAUCE

2 garlic cloves	½ cup olive oil	Salt and pepper
2 pounds tomatoes, quartered	2 tablespoons basil, plus more for garnish	

1. **BLEND.** Put the garlic, tomatoes, oil, and basil in a food processor, and season with salt and pepper. Pulse a few times to chop up and blend the ingredients, but do not puree. Pour into a large serving bowl.

2. **BOIL.** Bring a large pot of salted water to a boil. Add the pasta, stir vigorously, and cook for 1 minute. Strain, reserving ¼ cup of the pasta water.

3. **SAUCE.** Add the capellini to the bowl along with the reserved pasta water. Stir to coat. Garnish with roughly chopped basil leaves.

Tagliatelle with Pistachio-Artichoke Pesto

SERVES 4 | PREP 30 MIN | COOK 10 MIN

Pesto comes in many forms: it can be any blended sauce made with fresh herbs, nuts, oil, and cheese. Pistachio pesto is popular in Sicily, where pistachios are plentiful. Adding artichokes, another regional favorite, creates more depth of flavor.

FOR THE TAGLIATELLE

1 Egg Pasta Dough recipe (page 32)

1. **MAKE THE DOUGH.** Make the Egg Pasta Dough.

2. **THIN AND CUT.** Thin the pasta sheets until you can just see your fingers through them. Rub flour liberally on each side of the sheets. Using the wide cutter on the pasta machine, run the sheets through to cut, or use a knife to cut into ¼-inch strips.

FOR THE SAUCE

½ cup unsalted, shelled pistachios

½ cup artichoke hearts

½ cup tightly packed spinach leaves

½ cup grated Pecorino

1 garlic clove

½ cup olive oil

Salt and pepper

1. **BLEND.** Put the pistachios, artichoke hearts, spinach, Pecorino, and garlic in a food processor. With the machine running, slowly pour in the olive oil and run until the pesto is smooth. Season with salt and pepper to taste.

2. **BOIL.** Bring a large pot of salted water to a boil. Add the pasta, stir, and cook 2 minutes. Strain, reserving ½ cup of the pasta water.

3. **SAUCE.** In a large sauté pan over low heat, warm 1½ cups of the pesto 2 minutes. Add the tagliatelle and the reserved pasta water to the pan. Stir to coat.

TOOLS

Tools for Egg Pasta Dough (page 32)

Pasta machine

Knife

Food processor or blender

Large stockpot

Large sauté pan

Whole-Wheat Fettuccine Boscaiola

SERVES 4 | PREP 15 MIN | COOK 15 MIN

Many pastas are based on regional ingredients and named for the workers they were typically made for. "Bosco" means "woods," and "boscaiola" translates to "woodsman's wife." This dish is based on mushrooms foraged from the woods, but any mushrooms will work. This creamy, filling dish complements a heartier whole-wheat pasta dough.

TOOLS

Tools for Whole-Wheat Flour Pasta Dough (page 34)

Pasta machine

Knife

Large sauté pan

Large stockpot

FOR THE FETTUCCINE

1 Whole-Wheat Flour Pasta Dough recipe (page 34)

1. **MAKE THE DOUGH.** Make the Whole-Wheat Pasta Dough.

2. **THIN AND CUT.** Thin the pasta sheets until just before you can see your fingers through them. Rub flour liberally on each side of the sheets. Using the wide cutter on the pasta machine, run the sheets through to cut, or use a knife to cut into ⅓-inch strips.

FOR THE SAUCE

1 tablespoon olive oil	½ pound mushrooms, chopped	½ cup cream
½ pound ground sweet Italian sausage		Salt and pepper

1. **COOK.** In a large sauté pan with the oil over medium-high heat, cook the sausage until browned, 8 to 10 minutes. Add the mushrooms and cook for an additional 5 minutes over low heat until soft, stirring often.

2. **BOIL.** Bring a large pot of salted water to a boil. Add the pasta, stir, and cook 2 minutes. Strain, reserving ½ cup of the pasta water.

3. **SAUCE.** Keeping the heat on low, add the cream, pasta, and reserved pasta water to the pan with the mushrooms and sausage. Stir to coat, and season with salt and pepper to taste.

> **TIP:** Instead of straining the pasta into the sink, you can use tongs to transfer the pasta to the pan. Always reserve an extra cup of pasta water to add to the sauce as needed.

Paglia e Fieno with Prosciutto-Arugula Pink Sauce

SERVES 4 | PREP 30 MIN | COOK 10 MIN

Paglia e fieno is a mix of fresh egg and spinach-flavored egg fettuccine—it means "straw and hay" in Italian. The sauce is adapted from one I learned in the pasta classes I took in Bologna with the Tori family from Bluone in Italy Food & Wine Tours.

FOR THE PAGLIA E FIENO

½ Egg Pasta Dough recipe (page 32)
½ Flavored Pasta Dough recipe (page 38)

TOOLS

Tools for Egg Pasta Dough (page 32)

Pasta machine

Knife

Large sauté pan

Large stockpot

1. **MAKE THE DOUGH.** Make the Egg Pasta Dough. Make the Flavored Pasta Dough with the suggested spinach flavor.

2. **THIN AND CUT.** Thin the pasta sheets until you can just see your fingers through them. Rub flour liberally on each side of the sheets. Using the wide cutter on the pasta machine, run the sheets through to cut, or use a knife to cut into ⅓-inch strips.

continued

2 tablespoons olive oil

8 ounces prosciutto
or speck, cut into
cubes or strips

1 (14-ounce) can
crushed tomatoes

Salt and pepper

½ cup cream

1 tablespoon butter

2 cups arugula

1. **COOK.** In a large sauté pan with the oil, cook the prosciutto over medium heat 1 to 2 minutes until lightly browned. Add the tomatoes, and season with salt and pepper. Cook 5 minutes over medium heat.

2. **BOIL.** Bring a large pot of salted water to a boil. Add the pastas, stir, and cook 2 to 3 minutes. Strain.

3. **SAUCE.** Stir the cream into the tomatoes and cook for 1 minute. Add the butter and stir until melted. Add the pasta, stir to coat, and simmer 2 minutes. Top with the arugula.

TIP: When rolling out the spinach dough, you may need a little more flour for dusting and kneading to help absorb the extra moisture from the spinach.

Lagane and Ceci

SERVES 4 | PREP 30 MIN | COOK 30 MIN

Lagane, a thick, short, and wide ribbon of pasta made with durum wheat, is one of the oldest types of pasta, with origins in the Roman Empire. This chickpea stew-like sauce is very popular in Southern Italy, from Calabria to Puglia. This version is brothier than the traditional dish, and perfect for dipping crusty bread.

FOR THE LAGANE

½ Semola Rimacinata Pasta Dough recipe (page 37)

TOOLS
Tools for Semola Rimacinata Pasta Dough (page 37)

Pasta machine

Knife

Large stockpot

1. **MAKE THE DOUGH.** Make the Semola Rimacinata Pasta Dough.

2. **THIN AND CUT.** Roll out the dough to number 5 or 6 on the pasta machine dial—lagane should be thicker than tagliatelle. Rub flour liberally on each side of the sheets. Use a knife to cut into strips that are ¾ inch wide and 4 inches long.

FOR THE SAUCE

¼ cup olive oil

2 garlic cloves, minced

1 teaspoon minced fresh rosemary

Pinch of red pepper flakes (optional)

1 (14.5-ounce) can diced tomatoes

Salt and pepper

1 (15.5-ounce) can chickpeas

1 bay leaf

1. **SIMMER.** In a large stockpot over medium heat, sauté the oil, garlic, rosemary, and red pepper flakes (if using) 2 minutes. Add the tomatoes with their juices and season with salt and pepper. Bring the pot to a simmer, and add the chickpeas with their liquid, plus 1 full can of water and the bay leaf. Let simmer for 15 to 20 minutes, stirring often.

2. **BOIL.** Season the broth with salt and pepper if needed. Bring the broth to a boil. Add the lagane, and stir so they do not stick. Cook 2 to 3 minutes, until the pasta is cooked and remove the bay leaf. This will look like a creamy, starchy soup that will thicken as it cools.

Black Pepper Linguine with Red Clam Sauce

SERVES 4 | PREP 30 MIN | COOK 15 MIN

This classic recipe from Naples is very easy to make if you have fresh clams. This version is adapted from a recipe by Mary Ann Esposito of Ciao Italia, the longest-running cooking show in the United States.

TOOLS
Tools for
Flavored
Pasta Dough
(page 38)

Pasta
machine

Knife

Large
sauté pan

Large
stockpot

FOR THE LINGUINE

1 Flavored Pasta Dough recipe (page 38)
1 to 2 tablespoons black pepper

1. **MAKE THE DOUGH.** Make the Flavored Pasta Dough, replacing the spinach with black pepper. If you like more peppery flavor, add up to 2 tablespoons of pepper.

2. **THIN AND CUT.** Roll out the dough to number 5 or 6 on the pasta machine dial—linguine should be thicker than tagliatelle. Rub flour liberally on each side of the sheets. Use a knife to cut into strips ⅛ inch wide.

FOR THE SAUCE

4 pounds littleneck or mahogany clams in their shells, scrubbed
½ cup olive oil, divided

3 garlic cloves, minced
Pinch red pepper flakes (optional)
1 (28-ounce) can crushed tomatoes

Salt and pepper
2 tablespoons chopped parsley

1. **STEAM.** Put the clams in a large sauté pan with ¼ cup of olive oil. Cover and cook over medium heat until the clams open, about 5 minutes. Discard any that remain closed. Remove the clams from their shells. Reserve the clam juice.

2. **SIMMER.** Add the remaining ¼ cup of oil, the garlic, and the red pepper flakes (if using) to the pan and cook over medium heat until the garlic is softened, 5 minutes. Add the tomatoes and simmer 5 minutes. Season with salt and pepper. Add the reserved clam juice and simmer until the sauce thickens, 4 to 5 minutes.

3. **BOIL.** Bring a large pot of salted water to a boil. Add the pasta, stir, and cook 2 to 3 minutes. Strain.

4. **SAUCE.** Add the clams and linguine to the sauté pan. Toss to coat, and garnish with parsley.

> **TIP:** Make sure you find fresh clams for this recipe, not canned. As Italians would say, "If you don't have the right ingredients, make something else."

Herbed Pappardelle with Mushroom Ragù

SERVES 4 | PREP 30 MIN | COOK 15 MIN

Pappardelle are flat pasta ribbons originating from Tuscany. This thin, wide pasta works well with the rich, thick sauces popular in the region. A few handfuls of chopped fresh or dried herbs (rosemary, oregano, parsley, sage, basil, or thyme) in the dough complement the flavors of the mushroom ragù.

TOOLS

Tools for
Flavored
Pasta Dough
(page 38)

Pasta
machine

Knife or
pastry wheel

Large
sauté pan

Large
stockpot

FOR THE PAPPARDELLE

1 Flavored Pasta Dough recipe (page 38)
2 tablespoons minced fresh or dried herbs

1. **MAKE THE DOUGH.** Make the Flavored Pasta Dough, replacing the spinach with fresh herbs.

2. **THIN AND CUT.** Thin the pasta sheets until you can see your fingers through them. Rub flour liberally on each side of the sheets. Use a knife or pastry wheel to cut into 1-inch strips. Toss with flour and let the pasta sit on the counter to dry slightly, 10 minutes.

FOR THE SAUCE

¼ cup olive oil

½ cup finely diced shallot

1½ pounds mixed mushrooms, diced

½ cup white wine

1½ teaspoons fresh thyme

Salt and pepper

¼ cup heavy cream

2 tablespoons butter

½ cup grated Parmesan

2 tablespoons chopped fresh parsley

1. **COOK.** In a large sauté pan with the oil, cook the shallot over medium heat until soft, 5 minutes. Add the mushrooms and cook 8 to 10 minutes, until the mushroom liquid evaporates. Add the wine and thyme, season with salt and pepper, and cook 5 minutes, until the wine evaporates. Add the cream, butter, and Parmesan, and simmer over low heat 2 to 3 minutes until warmed through.

2. **BOIL.** Bring a large pot of salted water to a boil. Add the pappardelle to the pot, stir, and cook 1 to 2 minutes. Strain.

3. **SAUCE.** Add the pappardelle to the pan and stir to coat. Garnish with parsley.

TIP: If you would prefer this to be a heartier red sauce, add 1 (14.5-ounce) can crushed tomatoes after the mushrooms are cooked, and simmer 10 minutes.

Whole-Wheat Alpine Linguine

SERVES 4 | PREP 30 MIN | COOK 20 MIN

The cuisine of the Swiss and Austrian Alps has influenced the food in nearby Italian regions. Heartier pastas with melty cheeses, winter vegetables, and smoked meats, flavored with sage and butter, are more prevalent in these alpine areas.

TOOLS

Tools for Whole-Wheat Flour Pasta Dough (page 34)

Pasta machine

Knife

Large sauté pan

Large stockpot

FOR THE LINGUINE

1 Whole-Wheat Flour Pasta Dough recipe (page 34)

1. **MAKE THE DOUGH.** Make the Whole-Wheat Pasta Dough.

2. **THIN AND CUT.** Roll out the dough to number 5 or 6 on the pasta machine dial—linguine should be thicker than tagliatelle. Rub flour liberally on each side of the sheets. Use a knife to cut into strips slightly less than ⅛ inch wide.

FOR THE SAUCE

4 tablespoons olive oil

4 ounces speck or prosciutto, cut into cubes or strips

½ cup minced shallot

1 garlic clove, minced

2 teaspoons minced fresh sage or thyme

1 pound Brussels sprouts, thinly sliced

Salt and pepper

1 cup dry white wine

2 tablespoons butter

2 cups grated Gruyère

1. **COOK.** In a large sauté pan with the olive oil, cook the speck over medium heat until browned, 5 minutes. Add the shallot, garlic, and sage or thyme, and cook 2 minutes. Adjust the heat to medium-high, add the Brussels sprouts, season with salt and pepper, and sauté until browned, 4 to 5 minutes. Add the wine and butter, stir, and let simmer 2 minutes to reduce by half.

2. **BOIL.** Bring a large pot of salted water to a boil. Add the linguine, stir, and cook 2 to 3 minutes. Strain, reserving ½ cup of the pasta water.

3. **SAUCE.** Add the linguine, reserved pasta water, and cheese to the pan and toss until the cheese is melted and all ingredients are combined.

> **TIP:** Pair this with a crisp, dry white wine, such as Pinot Grigio or the Austrian Grüner Veltliner.

Pasta e Fagioli with Gluten-Free Maltagliati

SERVES 4 | PREP 30 MIN | COOK 30 MIN

"Maltagliati" means "poorly cut" in Italian. This type of pasta is usually made from pieces of dough that are left over after making other pasta and cut into irregular shapes.

TOOLS

Tools for Gluten-Free Pasta Dough (page 35)

Pasta machine

Knife or pastry wheel

Large sauté pan

Large stockpot

FOR THE MALTAGLIATI

1 Gluten-Free Pasta Dough recipe (page 35)

1. **MAKE THE DOUGH.** Make the Gluten-Free Pasta Dough.

2. **THIN AND CUT.** Slice the dough into ¼-inch-thick pieces. Flour the slices liberally with gluten-free flour. Roll out the dough a little thick, typically to number 5 on the pasta machine dial. Lay out the sheets on a pasta board. Use a knife or pastry wheel to cut the pasta into irregularly shaped 1-inch pieces. Toss with flour and dry slightly on the counter, 10 minutes.

FOR THE SOUP

¼ cup olive oil

2 garlic cloves, sliced thin

Pinch red pepper flakes

½ cup finely chopped carrot

½ cup finely chopped celery

½ cup finely chopped onion

1 teaspoon minced fresh rosemary

1 (15.5-ounce) can cannellini beans

½ cup chopped tomatoes

3 cups chicken or vegetable broth

½ teaspoon salt

½ teaspoon black pepper

1 Parmesan rind (optional)

1 cup spinach

1. **COOK.** In a large sauté pan with the oil, cook the garlic and red pepper flakes over medium heat 2 to 3 minutes. Stir in the carrot, celery, onion, and rosemary. Cook, stirring often, until softened, 7 to 8 minutes. Add the beans and their liquid, tomatoes, broth, 1 cup of water, salt, pepper, and Parmesan rind (if using). Bring to a gentle simmer and cook 30 minutes, stirring in the spinach in the last 5 minutes. Remove the rind and discard.

2. **BOIL.** Bring a large pot of salted water to a boil. Stir in the maltagliati slowly to prevent the pasta from sticking together. Cook 3 to 4 minutes until al dente. Strain.

3. **SERVE.** Stir the pasta into the soup, and ladle into bowls to serve.

> **TIP:** The Parmesan rind adds a depth of flavor to the broth. If not using, you can stir in a little grated Parmesan prior to serving or add some on top.

Quadrucci Spring Vegetable Minestrone

SERVES 4 TO 6 | PREP 30 MIN | COOK 40 MIN

Quadrucci are little pasta squares that are used in broths and soups. You can use any dough you prefer for this recipe, as all make a very good soup pasta with this small shape.

TOOLS

Tools for Egg Pasta Dough (page 32)

Pasta machine

Knife or pastry wheel

Large stockpot

FOR THE QUADRUCCI

1 Egg Pasta Dough recipe (page 32)

1. **MAKE THE DOUGH.** Make the Egg Pasta Dough.

2. **THIN AND CUT.** Thin the pasta sheets until you can just see your fingers through them. Rub flour liberally on each side of the sheets. Use a knife or pastry wheel to cut into ½-inch strips, then cut again into ½-inch squares. Toss with flour.

FOR THE SOUP

2 tablespoons olive oil
2 garlic cloves, minced
½ cup diced onion
½ cup diced carrot
½ cup diced celery
½ pound potatoes, cubed
1 (15-ounce) can diced tomatoes

1 cup canned cannellini beans, drained
4 cups chicken or vegetable stock
1 Parmesan rind
½ teaspoon salt
½ teaspoon black pepper

1 cup chopped asparagus
1 cup peas
1 cup fresh spinach
½ cup grated Parmesan
5 to 6 basil leaves, chopped

1. **COOK.** In a large stockpot with the oil over medium heat, cook the garlic, onion, carrot, and celery until soft, 3 to 4 minutes. Add the potatoes and cook 2 minutes. Add the tomatoes, beans, stock, 3 cups of water, Parmesan rind, salt and pepper and simmer 30 minutes. Add the asparagus and peas and cook for another 5 minutes.

2. **BOIL.** Bring a large pot of salted water to a boil. Slowly stir in the quadrucci to prevent the pasta from sticking together. Cook 3 to 4 minutes until al dente. Strain and add to the stockpot.

3. **SERVE.** Stir in the spinach and grated Parmesan. Ladle into bowls and top with basil.

TIP: Add prosciutto, smoked ham, or speck to add a meaty flavor to this soup. Sauté with oil before adding in vegetables.

Gluten-Free Pappardelle with Eggplant and Tomato-Mint Sauce

SERVES 4 | PREP 30 MIN | COOK 20 MIN

Gluten-free dough works best with cut pasta shapes. You can substitute gluten-free dough in most of the recipes in this chapter. The long ribbons of pappardelle pair well with this chunky, mint-scented tomato sauce. The mint adds a subtle flavor to the sauce that pairs well with the eggplant.

TOOLS

Tools for Gluten-Free Pasta Dough (page 35)

Pasta machine

Knife or pastry wheel

Large saucepan

Large stockpot

FOR THE PAPPARDELLE

1 Gluten-Free Pasta Dough recipe (page 35)

1. **MAKE THE DOUGH.** Make the Gluten-Free Pasta Dough.

2. **THIN AND CUT.** Slice the dough into ¼-inch-thick pieces. Flour liberally with gluten-free flour. Roll out the dough a little thick, to number 5 or 6 on the pasta machine dial. Rub flour liberally on each side of the sheets. Use a knife or pastry wheel to cut into 1-inch strips. Toss the strips with flour.

FOR THE SAUCE

2 tablespoons olive oil
2 garlic cloves, minced
½ cup minced onion
1 pound eggplant, chopped

1 (28-ounce) can diced tomatoes
2 tablespoons minced fresh mint
1 teaspoon oregano

Salt and pepper
½ cup goat cheese, divided
2 tablespoons chopped fresh basil

1. **SAUTÉ.** In a saucepan with the oil over medium heat, sauté the garlic and onion until soft, 3 to 4 minutes. Add the eggplant and cook until soft, 5 to 6 minutes, stirring often. Add the tomatoes, mint, oregano, and salt and pepper, and simmer 15 to 20 minutes.

2. **BOIL.** Bring a large pot of salted water to a boil. Add the pappardelle, stir, and cook 2 to 3 minutes. Strain.

3. **SAUCE.** Turn off the heat, add ¼ cup of goat cheese to the saucepan, and stir into the sauce until melted. Add the cooked pappardelle and stir to coat. Top with the remaining ¼ cup of goat cheese and the basil.

> **TIP:** Since gluten-free dough doesn't have much elasticity, slicing the dough into ¼-inch-thick sections and running these through the pasta machine helps get the dough into a sheet that can be cut. You do need to dust it with gluten-free flour to keep it from sticking.

Trenette al Pesto

SERVES 4 | PREP 30 MIN | COOK 10 MIN

Trenette is a narrow, flat pasta similar to linguine. It comes from the Liguria region, which is why it is most commonly paired with the famous basil pesto from Genoa. The addition of green beans and potatoes makes for a more filling dish.

TOOLS

Tools for Egg
Pasta Dough
(page 32)

Pasta
machine

Knife or
pastry wheel

Large
stockpot

Food
processor
or blender

Large bowl

FOR THE TRENETTE

1 Egg Pasta Dough
recipe (page 32)

½ pound baby
red-skinned
potatoes, halved

½ pound green beans

1. **MAKE THE DOUGH.** Make the Egg Pasta Dough.

2. **THIN AND CUT.** Thin the pasta sheets until just before you can see your fingers through them. Rub flour liberally on each side of the sheets. Use a knife or pastry wheel to cut into strips approximately ⅛ inch wide.

3. **BOIL.** Bring a large pot of salted water to a boil. Add the potatoes and cook 10 to 12 minutes, until just starting to get soft. Add the green beans and cook 3 minutes, then add the pasta and cook 2 to 3 more minutes. Strain, reserving ¼ cup of the pasta water.

2 cups fresh
basil leaves,
tightly packed

¼ cup grated
Parmesan, plus
more for serving

3 tablespoons
pine nuts

1 garlic clove

Salt and pepper

½ cup extra-virgin
olive oil

1. **BLEND.** Put the basil, Parmesan, pine nuts, and garlic in a food processor. Pulse a few times, then add salt and pepper to taste. With the machine running, slowly pour in the olive oil and run until the pesto is smooth.

2. **SAUCE.** Put the pesto in a large bowl, then add the strained pasta, potatoes, beans, and pasta water. Stir to coat.

TIP: Since pesto has such an assertive flavor, wine pairings can be difficult. Try this pasta with a light-bodied Vermentino. This minerally white is made from grapes grown on the Ligurian coast.

Gluten-Free Capellini with Lemon-Garlic Shrimp

SERVES 4 TO 6 | PREP 30 MIN | COOK 10 MIN

This light, flavorful sauce with shrimp is a perfect pairing with thin capellini. This restaurant-quality meal cooks quickly and will become a favorite. Pair it with a crisp white wine to complement the lemon and garlic flavors.

TOOLS

Tools for Gluten-Free Pasta Dough (page 35)

Pasta machine

Knife

Large sauté pan

Large stockpot

FOR THE CAPELLINI

1 Gluten-Free Pasta Dough recipe (page 35)

1. **MAKE THE DOUGH.** Make the Gluten-Free Pasta Dough.

2. **THIN AND CUT.** Slice the dough into ¼-inch-thick pieces. Flour liberally with gluten-free flour. Roll out the dough thin, to number 7 or 8 on the pasta machine dial. Rub more flour liberally on each side of the sheets. Using the narrow cutter on the pasta machine, run the sheets through to cut, or use a knife to cut into strips less than ⅛ inch wide.

FOR THE SAUCE

½ cup (1 stick) butter	¼ cup freshly squeezed lemon juice	1 to 2 tablespoons lemon zest
1 tablespoon garlic, minced	¼ cup white wine	2 tablespoons chopped Italian parsley
1 pound shrimp, cleaned with tails removed	½ teaspoon salt	
	½ teaspoon black pepper	

1. **SAUTÉ.** In a large sauté pan with the butter over medium heat, cook the garlic until softened, 3 to 4 minutes. Add the shrimp and cook until pink, 2 to 3 minutes.

2. **SIMMER.** Add the lemon juice and wine, season with salt and pepper, and simmer 2 minutes.

68   AUTHENTIC HOMEMADE PASTA

3. **BOIL.** Bring a large pot of salted water to a boil. Add the capellini, stir, and cook 1 minute. Strain.

4. **SAUCE.** Turn the heat to low, add the capellini, and stir to coat. Top with the lemon zest and parsley.

> **TIP:** Add a pinch of red pepper flakes to the butter and garlic to add some heat to this dish.

Reginette with Asparagus Cream

SERVES 4 | PREP 30 MIN | COOK 10 MIN

Reginette, or "little queens," are long, wide ribbons of pasta with ruffled edges. Traditionally this is a dry, factory-made pasta, but you can mimic this shape by using the fluted wheel of a pastry wheel to cut the wavy edges. The edges add a nice chewy texture.

TOOLS

Tools for
All-Purpose
Flour Pasta
Dough
(page 33)

Pasta
machine

Fluted pastry
wheel

Large
sauté pan

Knife

Food
processor
or blender

Large
stockpot

FOR THE REGINETTE

1 All-Purpose Flour Pasta Dough recipe (page 33)

1. **MAKE THE DOUGH.** Make the All-Purpose Flour Pasta Dough.

2. **THIN AND CUT.** Thin the pasta sheets until just before you can see your fingers through them. Rub flour liberally on each side of the sheets. Use a pastry wheel to cut into strips approximately ¾ inch wide.

FOR THE SAUCE

2 tablespoons olive oil	1 cup cream	Salt and pepper
¼ cup shallot, minced	½ cup grated	Lemon zest
1 pound asparagus	Parmesan	for garnish

1. **SAUTÉ.** In a large sauté pan with the oil over medium heat, cook the shallot until soft, 5 minutes. Cut the asparagus into 1-inch pieces, reserving the tops. Add the asparagus stems and cook on low heat until tender, 4 to 5 minutes. Add the cream and Parmesan and heat through 1 minute. Turn off the heat.

2. **BLEND.** Pour the mixture into a food processor, and blend until the asparagus is finely minced but not pureed. Season with salt and pepper to taste. Add the mixture back to the pan and keep warm on low heat.

3. **BOIL.** Bring a large pot of salted water to a boil. Add the reginette, stir, and cook 2 to 3 minutes. Strain.

4. **SAUCE.** Add the cooked pasta to the pan and combine over low heat until the pasta is coated with sauce. Add the asparagus tips and stir to combine. Garnish with lemon zest.

TIP: Topping this with pine nuts or chopped pistachios adds a nice, crunchy contrast.

Whole-Wheat Pizzoccheri Valtellina

SERVES 4 TO 6 | PREP 30 MIN | COOK 20 MIN

I learned about this pasta while visiting Lombardy, outside of Lago Maggiore. Francesca Settimi at Cook on the Lakes welcomed me into her beautiful home, kitchen, and garden to learn about recipes from Lombardy and Piedmont. While pizzoccheri is traditionally made with buckwheat pasta, whole-wheat pasta is a nice substitute.

TOOLS

Tools for Whole-Wheat Flour Pasta Dough (page 34)

Pasta machine

Knife or pastry wheel

Baking dish

Large stockpot

Large sauté pan

FOR THE PIZZOCCHERI

1 Whole-Wheat Flour Pasta Dough recipe (page 34)

1. **MAKE DOUGH.** Make the Whole-Wheat Pasta Dough.

2. **THIN AND CUT.** Roll out the dough thick, to number 3 or 4 on the pasta machine dial. Rub flour liberally on each side of the sheets. Use a knife or pastry wheel to cut into wide strips, about ½ inch by 2 inches.

FOR THE SAUCE

2 cups cubed potatoes

1 pound cabbage, chopped

8 tablespoons (1 stick) butter

2 garlic cloves

2 to 3 fresh sage leaves

Salt and pepper

1 cup shredded fontina

½ cup grated Parmesan

1. **PREHEAT.** Preheat the oven to 350°F, and grease the baking dish.

2. **BOIL.** Bring a large pot of salted water to a boil. Add the potatoes and boil 10 minutes. Add the cabbage and cook 5 minutes. Add the pasta and simmer 2 to 3 minutes. Strain.

3. **MELT.** In a large sauté pan with the butter over medium heat, cook the garlic and sage until they infuse the butter with flavor, 5 minutes.

4. **BAKE.** Strain the potatoes and cabbage and season with salt and pepper. Alternate layers of the pasta-potato-and-cabbage mixture, fontina cheese, and Parmesan in the baking dish. Pour the garlic butter on top and bake 10 to 15 minutes, or until the cheese starts to bubble.

> **TIP:** This cheesy, garlicky, buttery pasta is served at the ski resorts in the Alps near the Valtellina valley. Serve it with a light red Nebbiolo from Lombardy or Piedmont.

Sausage Lasagna

SERVES 4 | PREP 30 MIN | COOK 1 HR

This recipe is based on sagne chine, a lasagna from Calabria filled with tiny meatballs that is often served on Pasquetta, or Easter Monday. Here I used sliced sausage in place of the meatballs to save time.

TOOLS

Tools for All-Purpose Flour Pasta Dough (page 33)

Pasta machine

Knife or pastry wheel

Large stockpot

Large sauté pan

Baking dish

FOR THE PASTA

1 All-Purpose Flour Pasta Dough recipe (page 33)

1. **MAKE THE DOUGH.** Make the All-Purpose Flour Pasta Dough.

2. **THIN AND CUT.** Roll out the dough into sheets a little less than ⅛ inch thick. Rub flour liberally on each side of the sheets. Use a knife or pastry wheel to cut into 4-by-6-inch rectangles.

3. **BOIL.** Bring a large pot of salted water to a boil. Blanch the pasta rectangles 30 to 45 seconds, then plunge them into an ice bath. Drain on towels.

FOR THE LASAGNA

2 tablespoons olive oil, divided

2 garlic cloves, minced

Pinch red pepper flakes (optional)

1 (28-ounce) can crushed tomatoes

Salt and pepper

1 pound sweet or spicy Italian sausage links, sliced into ¼-inch rounds

2 large eggs, hard boiled and chopped

½ cup peas

½ cup shredded mozzarella

½ cup grated Pecorino, plus more for topping

½ pound ham, thinly sliced

1. **SAUTÉ.** In a large sauté pan over medium heat with 1 tablespoon of oil, cook the garlic and red pepper flakes (if using) until soft, 3 to 4 minutes. Add the tomatoes, season with salt and pepper, and cook 15 to 20 minutes.

2. **COOK.** In a separate sauté pan over medium-high heat with 1 tablespoon of oil, cook the sausage until browned, 8 to 10 minutes.

3. **ASSEMBLE.** Preheat the oven to 350°F. Cover the bottom of a large baking dish with sauce. Add the following in layers, using one-third of each filling: pasta rectangles, sausage, hard-boiled eggs, peas, mozzarella, Pecorino, ham, and sauce. Repeat two more times. Top with pasta rectangles, followed by the remaining sauce and cheese.

4. **BAKE.** Cover with foil and bake 45 to 50 minutes. Uncover and broil for 1 to 2 minutes to brown. Let rest for 10 to 15 minutes before slicing and serving.

> **TIP:** The variations on lasagna are limitless: substitute any of the fillings with your favorite meats or vegetables.

CHAPTER 5

Hand-Shaped Pasta

Foglie d'Ulivo with Spicy Tomato and Olive Sauce, page 102

Orecchiette

SERVES 4 | PREP 20 MIN

In Old Bari, in Puglia, there is an alleyway where women make this chewy, ear-shaped pasta all day. It takes some practice to get the right pressure to form the orecchiette. Some may tear and turn into lumps, but eventually you will be rolling them out like the ladies in Bari.

TOOLS

Tools for Semola Rimacinata Pasta Dough (page 37)

Butter knife

INGREDIENTS

1 Semola Rimacinata Pasta Dough recipe (page 37)

1. **MAKE THE DOUGH.** Make the Semola Rimacinata Pasta Dough. Divide the dough into quarters, and wrap three of the quarters in plastic so you can work in batches.

2. **ROLL AND CUT.** Starting at the center of the dough, use your hands to roll and stretch the dough back and forth away from you on the pasta board to form a ½-inch-thick rope. Cut the rope into ¼-inch-thick disks.

3. **SHAPE.** Place the smooth side of the butter knife on top of one disk and drag the dough by pushing down and pulling the knife toward you at the same time. This will thin the center of the dough and also curl it around the knife. Flip the curled dough inside out around the tip of your thumb so the rough edge is on top and it is shaped into a dome. The outside edges should have a ring of thicker dough surrounding a thin, rough-textured center.

4. **FLOUR.** Spread the orecchiette in a single layer and flour, so they do not stick together. Repeat with the rest of the disks, then repeat steps 2 and 3 three more times with the remaining wrapped dough.

TIP: When rolling out the rope, make sure to scrape your pasta board clean of flour. Any flour on the board will remove the friction needed to roll the dough and it will slide along the board instead of rolling.

ROLL TO STRETCH

CUT

DRAG TO SHAPE

FLIP TO SHAPE

FLOUR

Pici

SERVES 4 | PREP 20 MIN

Pici is a thick, hand-rolled pasta that resembles fat spaghetti. It's good to learn how to make strand-like pastas with just your hands. It's also a great project to do with kids. Pici comes from Siena in Toscana, and is traditionally served with a breadcrumb and olive oil sauce or a garlicky tomato sauce.

TOOLS

Tools for
All-Purpose
Flour Pasta
Dough
(page 33)

Rolling pin

Knife or
pastry wheel

INGREDIENTS

1 All-Purpose Flour Pasta Dough recipe (page 33)

1. **MAKE THE DOUGH.** Make the All-Purpose Flour Pasta Dough.

2. **ROLL AND CUT.** Using a rolling pin, roll out the dough into a ⅛-inch-thick rectangle. Use a knife or pastry wheel to cut into ¼-inch-wide strips.

3. **SHAPE.** Taking one strip of dough at a time, starting at the center, use your hands to roll and stretch the dough back and forth away from you on the pasta board. Form a thin rope about 10 inches long, resembling thick spaghetti.

4. **FLOUR.** Spread the pici in a single layer and flour, so they do not stick together.

> **TIP:** This is a wetter dough, and the pici will want to stick together. Lay them out flat with flour before cooking. You can also twirl them into very loose nests once you have tossed them in a lot of flour and freeze for later use.

ROLL

CUT

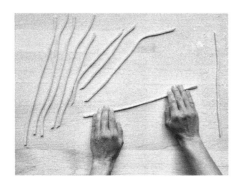

ROLL TO SHAPE

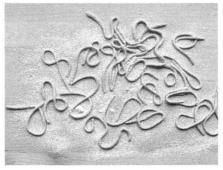

FLOUR

Orecchiette with Garlic-Broccoli Sauce

SERVES 4 | PREP 30 MIN | COOK 10 MIN

This is a great potluck meal for backyard parties and picnics, since it tastes great at room temperature. The raw broccoli steams quickly in the hot pasta water, and the Pecorino makes the sauce creamy. This is a garlicky sauce: you can add fewer garlic cloves if you prefer.

TOOLS

Tools for Semola Rimacinata Pasta Dough (page 37)

Butter knife

Large sauté pan

Large stockpot

FOR THE ORECCHIETTE

1 Semola Rimacinata Pasta Dough recipe (page 37)

1. **MAKE THE DOUGH.** Make the Semola Rimacinata Pasta Dough. Divide the dough into quarters, and wrap three of the quarters in plastic so you can work in batches.

2. **ROLL AND CUT.** Starting at the center of the dough, use your hands to roll and stretch the dough back and forth away from you on the pasta board to form a ½-inch-thick rope. Cut the rope into ¼-inch-thick disks.

3. **SHAPE.** Shape the orecchiette in batches, using the smooth side of a butter knife, and then flip and curl them around the tip of your thumb so the rough edge is on top and it is shaped into a dome. Spread the pasta in a single layer and flour. Repeat steps 2 and 3 with the remaining wrapped dough.

3 tablespoons olive oil

4 garlic cloves, minced

Pinch red pepper
flakes (optional)

1 large broccoli crown
or 1 (12-ounce) bag
broccoli florets,
finely chopped

1 cup grated Pecorino

Salt and pepper

1. **SAUTÉ.** In a large sauté pan with the oil, cook the garlic and red pepper flakes (if using) over medium heat until soft, 3 to 4 minutes. Add the broccoli and heat through.

2. **BOIL.** Bring a large pot of salted water to a boil. Add the orecchiette, simmer, and cook 3 to 4 minutes. Strain, reserving ¼ cup of the pasta water.

3. **SAUCE.** Turn off the heat and add the strained orecchiette to the pan with the reserved pasta water and the cheese. Stir until the sauce is creamy and the pasta is coated. Season with salt and pepper.

> **TIP:** This can also be made with crumbled sausage. Start by browning the sausage, then add the garlic and red pepper flakes and continue with the rest of the recipe.

Strozzapreti with Sausage and Broccoli Cream

SERVES 4 | PREP 30 MIN | COOK 10 MIN

The name of this pasta means "priest strangler," and there are a few stories as to where that name came from. The most popular is that priests in the Middle Ages were notorious for their gluttony, and ate pasta so greedily that they sometimes choked on it. Whatever its origin, this short, chewy pasta is easy to make.

TOOLS

Tools for All-Purpose Flour Pasta Dough (page 33)

Knife or pastry wheel

Large stockpot

Large sauté pan

Food processor or blender

FOR THE STROZZAPRETI

1 All-Purpose Flour Pasta Dough recipe (page 33)

1. **MAKE THE DOUGH.** Make the All-Purpose Flour Pasta Dough.

2. **ROLL AND CUT.** In two batches, use a rolling pin to roll out the dough to about ⅛ inch thick. Use a knife or pastry wheel to cut into 1-by-3-inch strips.

3. **SHAPE.** Taking one strip of dough at a time, rub it between your palms a few times to twist it into a rough spiral shape. Spread the pasta in a single layer and flour.

FOR THE SAUCE

1½ cups quartered potatoes

1½ cups broccoli florets

1 tablespoon olive oil

½ cup diced onion

12 ounces ground sweet Italian sausage

¾ cup grated Parmesan

Salt and pepper

1. **COOK.** Bring a large pot of water to a boil, add the potatoes, and cook 10 minutes. Add the broccoli and cook 2 to 3 minutes. Strain in a large sauté pan with the oil over medium heat, cook the onion until softened, 3 to 4 minutes. Add the sausage and cook until browned, 8 minutes.

2. **BOIL.** Bring a large pot of salted water to a boil. Add the strozzapreti, simmer, and cook 3 to 4 minutes. Strain, reserving 1 cup of the pasta water.

3. **BLEND.** Add the strained potatoes, broccoli, pasta water, and Parmesan to a food processor, and blend until smooth. Season with salt and pepper.

4. **SAUCE.** Add the pureed vegetables to the pan with the sausage. Add the strained pasta and stir to coat.

> **TIP:** This can be made vegetarian by omitting the sausage and just adding the pureed vegetables to the pasta.

Pici all'Aglione

SERVES 4 | PREP 30 MIN | COOK 10 MIN

"Aglione" means "big garlic" in Italian, and this dish is named after a locally grown garlic in Siena. You can use any garlic, and add as much or as little as you dare!

TOOLS

Tools for Semola Rimacinata Pasta Dough (page 37)

Rolling pin

Knife or pastry wheel

Large sauté pan

Large stockpot

FOR THE PICI

1 All-Purpose Flour Pasta Dough recipe (page 33)

1. **MAKE THE DOUGH.** Make the All-Purpose Flour Pasta Dough.

2. **ROLL AND CUT.** Using a rolling pin, roll out the dough into a ⅛-inch-thick rectangle. Use a knife or pastry wheel to cut into ¼-inch-wide strips.

3. **SHAPE.** Taking one strip of dough at a time, starting at the center, use your hands to roll and stretch the dough back and forth away from you on the pasta board. Form a thin rope about 10 inches long, resembling thick spaghetti. Spread the pasta in a single layer and flour.

FOR THE SAUCE

½ cup olive oil

4 to 6 garlic cloves, sliced thin

Pinch red pepper flakes (optional)

1 (28-ounce) can crushed tomatoes or 3 cups diced fresh plum tomatoes

Salt and pepper

1. **SAUTÉ.** In a large sauté pan with the oil, simmer the garlic and red pepper flakes (if using) on low heat to infuse the oil with garlic flavor. Add the tomatoes, season with salt and pepper, and cook over medium-high heat 8 to 10 minutes, stirring often.

2. **BOIL.** Bring a large pot of salted water to a boil. Add the pici, simmer, and cook 3 to 4 minutes. Strain.

3. **SAUCE.** Add the strained pici to the pan and stir to coat.

Busiate with Pesto alla Trapanese

SERVES 4 | PREP 30 MIN | COOK 10 MIN

This handmade pasta resembling corkscrews and its sauce are both from Sicily. The pesto is made of typically Sicilian ingredients—tomatoes, almonds, and garlic. The name comes from the word "busa," which refers to a knitting needle used to shape the pasta.

FOR THE BUSIATE

1 Semola Rimacinata Pasta Dough recipe (page 37)

1. **MAKE THE DOUGH.** Make the Semola Rimacinata Pasta Dough.

2. **ROLL AND SHAPE.** Pinch off a ½-inch piece of dough. Use your hands to roll the dough back and forth away from you on the pasta board to form a long, thin rope about ⅛ inch thick. Cut the rope into 3-inch pieces. Loosely roll the dough around the dowel, forming a spiral shape, then lightly roll the dowel with your palm against the board to create a thin corkscrew shape. Slide the busiate off the dowel. Spread the pasta in a single layer and flour.

FOR THE SAUCE

¾ pound cherry tomatoes

½ cup fresh basil leaves

½ cup almonds

1 garlic clove

½ cup grated Pecorino

½ cup olive oil

Salt and pepper

1. **BLEND.** Put the tomatoes, basil, almonds, garlic, and cheese in a food processor. Pulse a few times to chop. With the machine running, slowly pour in the olive oil and run until the pesto is smooth. Season with salt and pepper.

2. **BOIL.** Bring a large pot of salted water to a boil. Add the busiate and cook 3 to 4 minutes. Strain.

3. **SAUCE.** Put the pesto in a bowl with the strained pasta. Stir to coat.

TOOLS

Tools for Semola Rimacinata Pasta Dough (page 37)

⅛-inch dowel or knitting needle

Food processor or blender

Large stockpot

Large bowl

Spinach Garganelli with Prosciutto

SERVES 4 | PREP 30 MIN | COOK 10 MIN

Garganelli are from Emilia-Romagna and are made with fresh egg dough. They resemble ridged penne, but are made by hand using a gnocchi board. The legend behind this shape is that during the Middle Ages a chef had run out of filling for cappelletti, and instead rolled the pasta squares into tubes to serve with sauce.

TOOLS

Tools for Egg Pasta Dough (page 32)

Pasta machine or rolling pin

Knife or pastry wheel

Gnocchi board with ¼-inch round dowel

Large sauté pan

Large stockpot

FOR THE GARGANELLI
1 Flavored Pasta Dough recipe (page 38)

1. **MAKE THE DOUGH.** Make the Flavored Pasta Dough.

2. **ROLL AND CUT.** Roll out a pasta sheet until you can just see your fingers through it. Rub flour liberally on each side of the sheet. Use a knife or pastry wheel to cut into 2-inch squares.

3. **SHAPE.** Orient the gnocchi board so that the ridges run away from you. Then place a pasta square on the gnocchi board with one tip pointing toward you. Place the dowel on the tip and fold the tip over the dowel, rolling away from you to roll the dough around the dowel to make a tube. Press down to make ridges and seal the opposite tip. Slide the garganelli off the dowel and repeat with remaining pasta.

2 tablespoons olive oil

1 cup diced prosciutto

1 cup peas

1 (14.5-ounce) can
  crushed tomatoes

Salt and pepper

½ cup heavy cream

1. **COOK.** In a large sauté pan with the oil over medium heat, cook the prosciutto until golden brown, 4 to 5 minutes. Add the peas and cook 2 to 3 minutes until heated through. Add the tomatoes and salt and pepper to taste, and simmer 5 to 10 minutes.

2. **BOIL.** Bring a large pot of salted water to a boil. Add the garganelli and cook 3 to 4 minutes. Strain, reserving 2 tablespoons of the pasta water.

3. **SAUCE.** Keep heat on low, and stir in the cream. Add the strained pasta and the reserved pasta water and stir to coat.

> **TIP:** You can omit the tomatoes if you prefer this to be a cream sauce. Double the amount of cream and add ½ cup of Parmesan with the cream.

Basil Farfalle with Ricotta and Cherry Tomatoes

SERVES 4 | PREP 30 MIN | COOK 10 MIN

Farfalle means "butterflies" in Italian. This shape is also known as bow ties or strichetti. Adding basil to the dough makes a bright green pasta with a subtle basil flavor. Since we are using tomatoes in the sauce, basil pasta is a perfect complement.

TOOLS

Tools for Flavored Pasta Dough (page 38)

Pasta machine or rolling pin

Knife or fluted pastry wheel

Large bowl

Large sauté pan

Large stockpot

FOR THE FARFALLE

1 Flavored Pasta Dough recipe (page 38)
¼ cup chopped basil

1. **MAKE THE DOUGH.** Make the Flavored Pasta Dough, replacing the spinach with the basil.

2. **SHAPE.** Using the pasta machine or a rolling pin, roll out the dough to ⅛ inch thick. Use a knife to cut into 1-by-2-inch rectangles, or for wavy edges, use the fluted pastry wheel. Using your thumb and index finger, pinch the middle of the rectangle to form a ridge in the center; then pinch the edges into the center to make a butterfly shape.

FOR THE SAUCE

½ cup whole-milk ricotta	¼ cup pistachios	2 tablespoons olive oil
6 to 8 basil leaves, minced	½ cup grated Parmesan	1 garlic clove, minced
	Salt and pepper	1 cup cherry tomatoes, halved

1. **MIX.** In a large bowl, mix together the ricotta, basil, pistachios, and Parmesan. Season with salt and pepper.

2. **COOK.** In a large sauté pan with the oil over medium heat, cook the garlic 2 to 3 minutes, then add the cherry tomatoes and salt and pepper and cook 5 minutes or until the tomatoes start to burst.

3. **BOIL.** Bring a large pot of salted water to a boil. Add the farfalle and cook 2 to 3 minutes. Strain, reserving ¼ cup of the pasta water.

4. **SAUCE.** Add the strained pasta, the ricotta mixture, and 2 tablespoons of pasta water to the pan with the tomatoes and stir until the ricotta forms a creamy sauce. Add more pasta water if needed to thin out the sauce.

> **TIP:** You can make this a tricolor pasta by making three versions of the dough—plain egg (yellow), basil (green), and tomato paste (red). Cook together for a colorful meal. You can freeze the extra farfalle flat on a sheet pan and then transfer to bags.

Trofie with Basil-Pecan Pesto

SERVES 4 | PREP 30 MIN | COOK 10 MIN

Trofie is a short, thin, twisted pasta popular in Liguria. The spiral shape works well with pesto sauces. Don't give up if you aren't getting a nice spiral at first—you will get the hang of how much pressure to use after a few tries.

FOR THE TROFIE

1 All-Purpose Flour Pasta Dough recipe (page 33)

TOOLS

Tools for All-Purpose Flour Pasta Dough (page 33)

Food processor or blender

Large stockpot

Large bowl

1. **MAKE THE DOUGH.** Make the All-Purpose Flour Pasta Dough.

2. **ROLL.** In batches, pinch off ¼-inch pieces of dough. Use your hands to roll the dough back and forth away from you on the pasta board to form a tapered roll of dough ⅛ inch thick by 1 to 2 inches long.

3. **SHAPE.** Place a pastry scraper on top of the pasta piece at a 45-degree angle. Using the scraper, pull the pasta toward you while pressing it lightly into the board. The pasta will roll into a twist a bit like a screw. Spread the pasta in a single layer and flour.

FOR THE SAUCE

1 cup fresh basil leaves
¼ cup pecans
1 garlic clove
¼ cup grated Pecorino

1 teaspoon freshly squeezed lemon juice

½ cup olive oil
Salt and pepper

1. **BLEND.** Put the basil, pecans, garlic, cheese, and lemon juice into a food processor. Pulse a few times to chop. With the machine running, slowly pour in the olive oil and run until the pesto is smooth. Season with salt and pepper.

2. **BOIL.** Bring a large pot of salted water to a boil. Add the trofie and cook 3 to 4 minutes. Strain.

3. **SAUCE.** Put the pesto in a bowl with the strained pasta. Stir to coat.

Corzetti with Marjoram-Walnut Pesto

SERVES 4 | PREP 30 MIN | COOK 10 MIN

Corzetti is a flat, coin-shaped pasta from Genoa that has been around since the Middle Ages. The coins are made with a corzetti stamp to create designs like crests or crosses. You can find corzetti stamps in most kitchen stores and online, and there are artisans who will carve you a custom stamp.

TOOLS

Tools for Egg Pasta Dough (page 32)

Pasta machine or rolling pin

Corzetti stamp

Food processor or blender

Large stockpot

Large bowl

FOR THE CORZETTI

1 Egg Pasta Dough recipe (page 32)

1. **MAKE THE DOUGH.** Make the Egg Pasta Dough.

2. **ROLL AND CUT.** Using the pasta machine or a rolling pin, roll out the dough a little less than ⅛ inch thick. Flour the sheet, press the top of the corzetti stamp into the dough, and then use the bottom piece of the stamp to cut out the circle around the stamp. Lay out the corzetti, dust with flour, and allow them to dry slightly before using.

FOR THE SAUCE

1½ cups walnuts

6 to 8 fresh marjoram leaves or 1 to 2 sage leaves

1 garlic clove

¾ cup grated Parmesan

½ cup olive oil

Salt and pepper

1. **BLEND.** Put the walnuts, marjoram, garlic, and cheese in a food processor. Pulse a few times to chop. With the machine running, slowly pour in the olive oil and run until the pesto is smooth. Season with salt and pepper.

2. **BOIL.** Bring a large pot of salted water to a boil. Add the corzetti and cook 2 to 3 minutes. Strain, reserving 1 to 2 tablespoons of the pasta water.

3. **SAUCE.** Put the pesto in a bowl with the strained pasta. Stir to coat. Add the pasta water to make the sauce creamy.

TIP: The pasta should be rolled a little thick to give the corzetti a bit of bite and to hold the shape of the stamp.

Fusilli al Ferretto with 'Nduja Sauce

SERVES 4 | PREP 30 MIN | COOK 10 MIN

Fusilli, also known as "maccheroni al ferretto," or in dialect "fileja," is an irregularly shaped pasta that resembles broken tubes. It's shaped by quickly rolling small pieces of dough around a thin iron rod (a "ferro" in Italian). 'Nduja is a soft, spicy salami that can be found in many grocery stores with a specialty cheese section.

TOOLS

Tools for Semola Rimacinata Pasta Dough (page 37)

Thin dowel or knitting needle

Large sauté pan

Large stockpot

FOR THE FUSILLI

1 Semola Rimacinata Pasta Dough recipe (page 37)

1. **MAKE THE DOUGH.** Make the Semola Rimacinata Pasta Dough.

2. **ROLL.** In batches, pinch off ½-inch pieces of dough. Use your hands to roll the dough back and forth away from you on the pasta board to form a long, thin rope about ¼ inch thick.

3. **SHAPE.** Center the dowel across the pasta and roll it back and forth a few times to thin the pasta slightly. Then wrap the dough around the dowel, and using a very light touch with two fingers, roll the dowel back and forth while stretching the dough along the dowel with your fingers. Repeat with the rest of the dough. Spread the pasta in a single layer and flour.

FOR THE SAUCE

½ cup 'nduja or very finely minced spicy salami

¼ cup grated Pecorino Romano

1. **COOK.** In a large sauté pan over low heat, cook the 'nduja 1 to 2 minutes.

2. **BOIL.** Bring a large pot of salted water to a boil. Add the fusilli and cook 2 to 3 minutes. Strain, reserving 2 tablespoons of the pasta water.

3. **SAUCE.** Add the strained pasta, the pasta water, and the Pecorino to the pan. Stir until the meat melts down and combines with the cheese to form a sauce.

> **TIP:** Each fusilli will look different—some will seal all the way and look like a tube, while others will only seal in spots. This is the fun of making handmade pasta! If your pasta is sticking to your dowel, lightly flour the dowel or use a lighter touch.

Anellini alla Pecorara

SERVES 4 | PREP 30 MIN | COOK 10 MIN

Anellini are small pasta rings that are fun to make fresh. Typically, these are dry, tiny rings used for soup pasta. Freshly made anellini are about ¾ of an inch in size and have a nice toothy texture. "Alla pecorara" means "shepherd's pasta," which is probably due to the ricotta topping. This a traditional vegetarian pasta sauce from Abruzzo.

TOOLS
Tools for
Semola
Rimacinata
Pasta Dough
(page 37)

Knife or
pastry wheel

Large
sauté pan

Large
stockpot

FOR THE ANELLINI

1 Semola Rimacinata Pasta Dough recipe (page 37)

1. **MAKE THE DOUGH.** Make the Semola Rimacinata Pasta Dough.

2. **ROLL AND CUT.** In batches, use your hands to roll the dough into ¼-inch-thick ropes. Use a knife or pastry wheel to cut into 2-inch pieces.

3. **SHAPE.** Wrap a dough piece around your index finger, forming a little ring. Make sure to press the ends together so they hold the shape. Spread the pasta in a single layer and flour.

FOR THE SAUCE

2 tablespoons olive oil
½ cup chopped onion
½ cup chopped carrot
½ cup chopped celery
1 cup diced eggplant

1 cup diced green
   bell pepper
1 cup diced zucchini
1 (28-ounce) can
   diced tomatoes

Salt and pepper
½ cup whole-milk
   ricotta
½ cup grated Pecorino

1. **SAUTÉ.** In a large sauté pan with the oil over medium heat, cook the onion, carrot, and celery until golden brown, 8 to 9 minutes. Add the eggplant, pepper, and zucchini, and cook 5 more minutes until soft. Add the tomatoes, season with salt and pepper, and let simmer 15 to 20 minutes.

2. **BOIL.** Bring a large pot of salted water to a boil. Add the anellini and cook 3 to 4 minutes. Strain.

3. **SAUCE.** Turn off the heat, add the strained pasta to the pan, and stir to coat. To serve, top each portion with a tablespoon or two of ricotta and Pecorino.

> **TIP:** This can be turned into a baked dish: after step 3, just pour the pasta and sauce into a baking dish, top with mozzarella, and bake at 350°F for 5 to 10 minutes, until the cheese is melted.

Capunti alla Pastora

SERVES 4 | PREP 30 MIN | COOK 10 MIN

This is another pasta from Southern Italy that is based on shepherds' food—"pastora" is another word for "shepherd." It is a mix of sausage, mushrooms, and ricotta. Capunti is a short pasta with indentations resembling an empty pea pod. It is a good shape to hold the crumbled sausage and diced mushrooms.

TOOLS
Tools for Semola Rimacinata Pasta Dough (page 37)

Knife or pastry wheel

Large sauté pan

Large stockpot

FOR THE CAPUNTI

1 Semola Rimacinata Pasta Dough recipe (page 37)

1. **MAKE THE DOUGH.** Make the Semola Rimacinata Pasta Dough.

2. **ROLL AND CUT.** Use your hands to roll the dough into a ½-inch-wide rope. Use a knife or pastry wheel to cut into ½-inch pieces. Roll each piece with your palm to round it out.

3. **SHAPE.** Using two fingers, press into the dough and drag it across the pasta board, leaving two indentations with your fingertips. Spread the pasta in a single layer and flour.

FOR THE SAUCE

1 tablespoon olive oil	1 cup diced mushrooms	Salt and pepper
¾ pound ground sweet Italian sausage	1 pound whole-milk ricotta	

1. **SAUTÉ.** In a large sauté pan with the oil over medium-high heat, brown the sausage 8 to 10 minutes. Drain all but 1 tablespoon of the fat and remove the sausage. Add the mushrooms to the same pan over medium heat and cook 5 minutes, until softened. Return the sausage to the pan.

2. **BOIL.** Bring a large pot of salted water to a boil. Add the capunti and cook 3 to 4 minutes. Strain, reserving 2 tablespoons of the pasta water.

3. **SAUCE.** Add the ricotta, strained pasta, and pasta water to the pan, and stir to combine until the cheese melts and turns into a creamy sauce. Season with salt and pepper.

TIP: Use a spicy Italian sausage or add ½ to 1 teaspoon red pepper flakes for a spicier flavor.

Foglie d'Ulivo with Spicy Tomato and Olive Sauce

SERVES 4 | PREP 30 MIN | COOK 10 MIN

Foglie d'ulivo is shaped like an olive leaf, and usually made with spinach in the dough. Similar to orecchiette, but a little larger and more oblong, this pasta also comes from Puglia.

TOOLS

Tools for Semola Rimacinata Pasta Dough (page 37)

Knife or pastry wheel

Butter knife

Large sauté pan

Large stockpot

FOR THE FOGLIE D'ULIVO

1 Semola Rimacinata Pasta Dough recipe (page 37)
½ cup minced spinach

1. **MAKE THE DOUGH.** Make the Semola Rimacinata Pasta Dough, adding the spinach to the water and kneading it into the dough to make a green pasta.

2. **ROLL AND CUT.** Using your hands, roll one-quarter of the dough into a ½-inch-wide rope. Let the remaining dough rest wrapped in plastic while you work on the first batch. In batches, use a knife or pastry wheel to cut the rope into ½-inch-thick disks.

3. **SHAPE.** Place the smooth back of the butter knife on top of a disk. Drag the dough toward you by pushing down while holding the tip of the dough with your other hand so you are stretching the pasta into a leaf shape. Spread the pasta in a single layer and flour.

¼ cup olive oil

2 to 3 garlic
cloves, minced

1 teaspoon red
pepper flakes

1 (28-ounce) can
crushed tomatoes

Salt and pepper

4 ounces goat
cheese, divided

½ cup Kalamata
olives, chopped

1. **COOK.** In a large sauté pan with the oil over medium heat, simmer the garlic and red pepper flakes 2 to 3 minutes. Add the tomatoes, season with salt and pepper, and simmer over medium-high heat 15 to 20 minutes.

2. **BOIL.** Bring a large pot of salted water to a boil. Add the pasta and cook 3 to 4 minutes. Strain.

3. **SAUCE.** Turn off the heat and stir 3 ounces of goat cheese and the olives to the tomato sauce. Add the strained pasta and stir to coat. Top with the remaining goat cheese.

> **TIP:** This can be made with crumbled sausage. Take the sausage out of its casing and brown it, then add garlic and red pepper flakes and continue with the rest of the recipe.

Lorighittas with Tomato, Chicken, and Saffron Sauce

SERVES 4 | PREP 30 MIN | COOK 50 MIN

This more complex pasta shape from Sardinia is worth the effort. Saffron is used in most tomato sauces in Sardinia; this one is a braised chicken sauce. Traditionally, the chicken pieces are taken out and eaten as a second course, but I like to shred the chicken meat into the sauce.

TOOLS

Tools for Semola Rimacinata Pasta Dough (page 37)

Large sauté pan

Large stockpot

FOR THE LORIGHITTAS

1 Semola Rimacinata Pasta Dough recipe (page 37)

1. **MAKE THE DOUGH.** Make the Semola Rimacinata Pasta Dough.

2. **ROLL.** In batches, pinch off 1-inch pieces of dough. Use your hands to roll and stretch the dough into a thin strand about ⅛ inch wide.

3. **SHAPE.** Wrap the dough around two of your fingers twice, sealing the loose ends and pinching off the extra dough. You now have two bands of pasta wrapped around your fingers. Twist the two bands around each other to form a braided ring. Repeat with the rest of the dough. Spread the pasta in a single layer and flour.

2 tablespoons olive oil

2 chicken thighs

2 chicken drumsticks

½ cup chopped onion

2 garlic cloves

1 (28-ounce) can
  crushed tomatoes

¼ teaspoon saffron

½ cup white wine

Salt and pepper

½ cup grated Pecorino

2 tablespoons
  chopped parsley

1. **SAUTÉ.** In a large sauté pan with the oil over medium heat, brown the chicken 10 to 12 minutes, until cooked through. Remove the chicken, add the onion and garlic, and cook until softened, 5 minutes. Add the tomatoes, saffron, and wine. Season with salt and pepper and cook 5 minutes. Return the chicken to the pan and simmer, covered, 30 to 40 minutes.

2. **BOIL.** Bring a large pot of salted water to a boil. Add the pasta and cook 3 to 4 minutes. Strain.

3. **SAUCE.** Remove the chicken from the pan, shred the thighs, and add them back to the sauce. Reserve the drumsticks for a second course. Add the strained pasta and stir to coat. Garnish with Pecorino and parsley.

> **TIP:** You can omit the saffron, but it is easy to find in very small jars and only a pinch is needed to add a subtle layer of flavor to this Sardinian sauce.

Cavatelli with Short Rib Ragù

SERVES 4 | PREP 30 MIN | COOK 2 HR 30 MIN

"Cavatelli" means "little caves," which refers to their indented shape. You'll use a gnocchi board to create the ridges on this pasta, which are perfect to hold rich sauces like this ragù.

TOOLS

Tools for Semola Rimacinata Pasta Dough (page 37)

Knife or pastry wheel

Gnocchi board or fork

Dutch oven

Large stockpot

FOR THE CAVATELLI

1 Semola Rimacinata Pasta Dough recipe (page 37)

1. **MAKE THE DOUGH.** Make the Semola Rimacinata Pasta Dough.

2. **ROLL AND CUT.** In batches, use your hands to roll one-quarter of the dough into a ½-inch-wide rope. Use a knife or pastry wheel to cut the rope into ⅓-inch sections.

3. **SHAPE.** Place one pasta piece on the gnocchi board. Using the side of your thumb, push down lightly and drag the pasta along the ridges of the board and curl it around the indentation from your thumb. Press as hard as you can without the pasta sticking since your goal is to thin the pasta slightly in the center so it cooks through. Spread the pasta in a single layer and flour.

FOR THE SAUCE

2 pounds short ribs	1 garlic clove	1 teaspoon minced rosemary
Salt and pepper	1 (14.5-ounce) can crushed tomatoes	1 teaspoon minced thyme
2 tablespoons olive oil	1 cup red wine	
½ cup minced carrot	1 cup beef broth	1 cup grated Parmesan
½ cup minced celery		
½ cup minced onion		

1. **COOK.** Preheat the oven to 325°F. Liberally season the ribs with salt and pepper. Heat the oil in a Dutch oven over medium heat and brown the ribs on all sides, about 10 minutes. Transfer the ribs to a bowl.

2. **SAUTÉ.** Add the carrot, celery, onion, and garlic to the Dutch oven, and cook over medium heat until soft and golden, 6 to 8 minutes.

3. **SIMMER.** Add the tomatoes, wine, broth, rosemary, thyme, and more salt and pepper and let simmer 10 minutes.

4. **BAKE.** Return the short ribs to the Dutch oven, cover, and bake 2 to 2½ hours, until tender. Remove the ribs from the sauce to cool. Remove the bones, shred the meat, and return the meat to the sauce.

5. **BOIL.** Bring a large pot of salted water to a boil. Add the cavatelli and cook 3 to 4 minutes. Strain.

6. **SAUCE.** Add the cavatelli to the sauce, and stir with Parmesan to coat.

> **TIP:** If you don't have a gnocchi board, you can also make smooth cavatelli by using your thumb to drag the dough along your pasta board to make the indentation.

CHAPTER 6

Stuffed Pasta

Raviolo al'Uovo, page 144

Ravioli

SERVES 4 | PREP 30 MIN

The simplest way to make beautiful, uniform ravioli is by using a ravioli mold. These are easy to find online and cost less than $20. They usually come with a small rolling pin, a metal mold, and a plastic press. The press makes the pockets for the filling. For this recipe, you'll practice with a simple ricotta filling.

TOOLS

Tools for Egg Pasta Dough (page 32)

Rolling pin or pasta machine

Ravioli press and mold

Knife or pastry wheel

Sheet pan

INGREDIENTS

1 Egg Pasta Dough recipe (page 32)

1 cup ricotta

¼ cup grated Parmesan

¼ teaspoon salt

1. **MAKE THE DOUGH.** Make the Egg Pasta Dough.

2. **CREATE THE FILLING.** Stir together the ricotta, Parmesan, and salt in a bowl until fully blended.

3. **THIN AND CUT.** On a floured surface, using a rolling pin or pasta machine, roll out one-quarter of the dough into a long sheet ¹⁄₁₆ inch thick. Wrap unused dough in plastic wrap so it doesn't dry out. Using the ravioli press as a guide to measure, use a knife or pastry wheel to cut the dough into two sheets a little longer and wider than the press. Roll out more dough as needed to make two equal sheets.

4. **FILL.** Liberally flour one side of a thinned pasta sheet. Lay it on top of the mold, floured-side down. Use the ravioli press to make pockets by pressing it down into the holes of the mold. Spoon 1 tablespoon of cheese filling into each pocket. Lay the second pasta sheet on top and stretch to cover the ravioli completely. Using a rolling pin, roll over the mold to cut and seal the ravioli. Remove the excess dough around the mold. Turn the mold upside down to release the ravioli. Repeat steps 2 through 4 three more times with the remaining dough and filling.

5. **FLOUR.** Place the ravioli in a single layer on a sheet pan, flour lightly, and cover to prevent from drying out, or freeze and transfer to plastic bags for later use.

MIX FILLING

THIN

FILL

ROLL TO SEAL

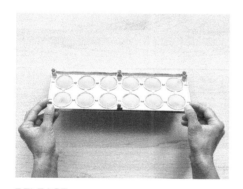

RELEASE

FLOUR

TIP: If you do not have a ravioli mold, you can use a ravioli stamp to cut and seal the pasta. These come in many shapes and sizes, from square to round to triangles. You can also use the tines of a fork to seal the sides of your ravioli.

Agnolotti del Plin

SERVES 4 | PREP 20 MIN

Agnolotti pasta rectangles are made by pinching the dough together to form little pockets of filling. "Plin" means "pinch" in the local dialect in Piedmont, where this pasta originates. For this Learn and Make recipe, you'll practice with a simple ricotta filling.

TOOLS

Tools for Egg Pasta Dough (page 32)

Pastry or resealable plastic bag

Rolling pin or pasta machine

Fluted pastry wheel

Sheet pan

INGREDIENTS

1 Egg Pasta Dough recipe (page 32)

1 cup ricotta

¼ cup grated Parmesan

¼ teaspoon salt

1. **MAKE THE DOUGH.** Make the Egg Pasta Dough.

2. **CREATE THE FILLING.** Stir together the ricotta, Parmesan, and salt in a bowl. Add to a pastry bag, and snip the end to create a ½-inch opening.

3. **THIN AND FILL.** On a floured surface, using a rolling pin or pasta machine, roll out one-quarter of the dough into a long sheet ¹⁄₁₆ inch thick. Wrap unused dough in plastic wrap so it doesn't dry out. Lay a long strip of dough on a floured pasta board and pipe filling along the lower third of the sheet. Fold the dough tightly over the filling so it forms a tube of filling covered by dough, leaving about an inch of dough in front of the filling overlapping the bottom sheet.

4. **PINCH.** Using your fingers, pinch the dough together every inch or so to separate and seal the filling into individual pockets.

5. **CUT.** Use the fluted pastry wheel to trim the extra dough, leaving about ½ inch of dough in front of the filling. Cut at each pinch, moving the fluted pastry wheel away from you. This forms a pillow of pasta with pinched edges. Repeat steps 3 through 5 three more times with the remaining dough and filling.

6. **FLOUR.** Place in a single layer on a sheet pan, flour lightly, and cover to prevent from drying out, or freeze and transfer to plastic bags for later use.

MIX FILLING

THIN

FILL

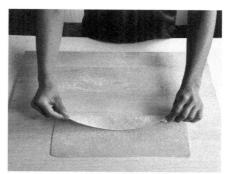

FOLD TO COVER

PINCH TO SEAL

CUT AND FLOUR

TIP: Traditionally, a meat filling is used for agnolotti, but you can use any firm filling that will stay inside the pinched pillow.

Lemon-Ricotta Ravioli with Butter-Parmesan Sauce

SERVES 4 TO 6 | PREP 30 MIN | COOK 10 MIN

This lemony ravioli is a customer favorite at Melina's Fresh Pasta. Serve this with a simple sauce that comes together quickly. The spinach dough is a nice complement to the lemon filling.

TOOLS

Tools for Flavored Pasta Dough (page 38)

Rolling pin

Ravioli mold with press

Large sauté pan

Large stockpot

FOR THE RAVIOLI

1 Flavored Pasta Dough recipe (page 38)

2 cups whole-milk ricotta

Zest of 2 lemons

1 tablespoon minced parsley

½ cup grated Parmesan

¼ teaspoon salt

1. **MAKE THE DOUGH.** Make the Flavored Pasta Dough.

2. **CREATE THE FILLING.** Stir together the ricotta, lemon zest, parsley, Parmesan, and salt in a mixing bowl until fully blended.

3. **THIN, CUT, AND FILL.** Use a rolling pin to roll out one-quarter of the dough into two ⅟₁₆-inch-thick sheets. Liberally flour one side of a pasta sheet. Lay it on top of the mold, floured-side down. Use the ravioli press to make pockets by pressing it down into the holes of the mold. Spoon about 1 tablespoon of cheese filling into each dough pocket. Lay a second pasta sheet on top and stretch to cover. Using a rolling pin, roll over the mold to cut and seal the ravioli, removing excess dough, and release the ravioli. Repeat three more times with the remaining dough and filling.

4 tablespoons salted butter
¼ cup grated Parmesan

1. **MELT.** In a large sauté pan, melt the butter on low heat.

2. **BOIL.** Bring a large pot of salted water to a boil. Add the ravioli and simmer 5 to 6 minutes, or until the ravioli float to the surface. Strain, reserving 2 tablespoons of the pasta water.

3. **SAUCE.** Turn off the heat. Add the Parmesan, strained ravioli, and reserved pasta water to the pan and stir to coat.

> **TIP:** Do not forget to flour the bottom pasta sheet, or the pasta will stick to the mold.

Burrata Agnolotti with Roasted Cherry Tomatoes

SERVES 4 | PREP 30 MIN | COOK 35 MIN

I'll never forget when I first discovered burrata: a ball of fresh mozzarella with a soft, creamy filling called stracciatella. Roasting cherry tomatoes concentrates their sweet flavor, which pairs well with this creamy filling.

TOOLS

Tools for Egg
Pasta Dough
(page 32)

Pastry or
resealable
plastic bag

Rolling pin

Fluted pastry
wheel

Sheet pan

Large
stockpot

Large
sauté pan

FOR THE AGNOLOTTI

1 Egg Pasta Dough recipe (page 32)	2 cups whole-milk ricotta	1 cup chopped burrata Pinch salt

1. **MAKE THE DOUGH.** Make the Egg Pasta Dough.

2. **CREATE THE FILLING.** In a large mixing bowl, stir together the ricotta, burrata, and salt. Add the mixture to the pastry bag.

3. **THIN, FILL, AND PINCH.** Use a rolling pin to roll out one-quarter of the dough into a long sheet $\frac{1}{16}$ inch thick. Pipe a continuous line of filling along the lower third of the sheet. Fold the dough tightly over the filling. Then pinch the dough together every inch or so to separate and seal.

4. **CUT.** Using a fluted pastry wheel, trim the extra dough and cut at each pinch into individual pieces. Repeat steps 3 and 4 three more times with the remaining dough and filling.

2 cups cherry or grape tomatoes, halved

2 tablespoons olive oil

1 garlic clove, minced

2 tablespoons fresh herbs, divided

Salt and pepper

1. **ROAST.** Preheat the oven to 400°F. Add the tomato halves to a well-oiled sheet pan. Drizzle the olive oil on top, sprinkle with the garlic and 1 tablespoon of herbs, season with salt and pepper, and bake 25 minutes.

2. **BOIL.** Bring a large pot of salted water to a boil. Add the agnolotti and simmer 3 to 4 minutes, or until the agnolotti float to the surface. Strain and set aside in a large sauté pan.

3. **SAUCE.** Remove the tomatoes from the sheet pan along with their juices and add to the pan with the agnolotti. Cook over medium heat 2 minutes and stir to coat. Garnish with the remaining 1 tablespoon of herbs.

TIP: Since roasting tomatoes brings out their sweetness, this is a great recipe for out-of-season tomatoes. In season, use heirloom cherry tomatoes if you can find them for a colorful contrast.

Culurgiones with Tomato Sauce

SERVES 4 | PREP 30 MIN | COOK 30 MIN

Culurgiones are a Sardinian pasta sealed together with what looks like stitches or a braid. It may take a few tries to get the hang of this pudgy pasta, but the effort is worth it!

FOR THE CULURGIONES

1 Semola Rimacinata Pasta Dough recipe (page 37)

2 cups peeled and quartered potatoes

1 garlic clove, minced

1 tablespoon olive oil, divided

1 tablespoon chopped mint leaves

½ cup grated Pecorino

Salt and pepper

TOOLS

Tools for Semola Rimacinata Pasta Dough (page 37)

Large stockpot

Large sauté pan

Large bowl

Rolling pin

Cookie cutter or large glass

1. **MAKE THE DOUGH.** Make the Semola Rimacinata Pasta Dough.

2. **CREATE THE FILLING.** Boil the potatoes until tender, 15 minutes. Meanwhile, sauté the garlic over medium heat in ½ tablespoon of olive oil until soft, 3 to 4 minutes. Strain the potatoes and place in a large bowl. Add the remaining ½ tablespoon of oil, the mint, and the Pecorino and mash until smooth. Season with salt and pepper to taste. Allow to cool.

3. **THIN AND FILL.** Use a rolling pin to roll out the dough between 1/16 and 1/8 inch thick. Cut 3-inch circles with a glass or cookie cutter. Spoon 1 tablespoon of filling in the center of each circle. Fold the dough over like a taco around the filling.

4. **PINCH.** Starting at one end of the taco, pinch the dough edges together to create a seal. As you move along, alternate sides as you pinch to create a zig-zag seal, like a braid. Repeat this until you get to the end and seal shut. Filling escaping the seal is a sign you've used the right amount.

continued

FOR THE SAUCE

2 tablespoons olive oil

2 garlic cloves, minced

Pinch red pepper flakes (optional)

1 (28-ounce) can crushed tomatoes

Salt and pepper

1. **SAUTÉ.** In a large sauté pan with the oil over medium heat, cook the garlic and red pepper flakes (if using) until soft, 2 to 3 minutes. Add the tomatoes, season with salt and pepper, and cook 15 to 20 minutes.

2. **BOIL.** Bring a large pot of salted water to a boil. Add the culurgiones and simmer 4 to 5 minutes. Strain.

3. **SAUCE.** Add the culurgiones to the pan, turn off the heat, and stir to coat.

TIP: You can add ¼ cup of goat cheese to the filling while the potatoes are hot for a tangier flavor.

Scarpinocc with Fontina in Butter Sauce

SERVES 4 | PREP 30 MIN | COOK 10 MIN

Scarpinocc is a uniquely shaped stuffed pasta from Northern Italy. It looks like a wooden clog and is based on the Italian word for "shoe": scarpa. Drizzle a little balsamic vinegar to finish this dish to help balance the sauce and buttery fontina cheese.

FOR THE SCARPINOCC

1 Egg Pasta Dough recipe (page 32)

1 cup diced Taleggio or fontina cheese

½ cup ricotta

¼ cup cream

Salt and pepper

TOOLS

Tools for Egg Pasta Dough (page 32)

Food processor or blender

Pastry or resealable plastic bag

Rolling pin

Knife or fluted pastry wheel

Large sauté pan

Large stockpot

1. **MAKE THE DOUGH.** Make the Egg Pasta Dough.

2. **CREATE THE FILLING.** In a food processor, blend the cheeses and cream. Season with salt and pepper. Spoon the filling into a pastry or resealable plastic bag.

3. **THIN, CUT, AND FILL.** Use a rolling pin to roll out two sheets of dough 1/16 inch thick. Use the knife or pastry wheel to cut the pasta into 2-by-2½-inch rectangles. Pipe 2 inches of filling in the center of the long side of each rectangle. Fold the pasta over the filling and seal. Pinch the ends of the pasta closed. Use your finger to press an indentation in the center of the pasta filling.

FOR THE SAUCE
¼ cup (½ stick) butter

1. **MELT.** In a large sauté pan, melt the butter over low heat.

2. **BOIL.** Bring a large pot of salted water to a boil. Add the scarpinocc and simmer 3 to 4 minutes. Strain, reserving 2 tablespoons of the pasta water.

3. **SAUCE.** Using a slotted spoon, transfer the scarpinocc to the pan. Add 2 tablespoons of the reserved pasta water, and cook 1 to 2 minutes over low heat until coated.

Gluten-Free Anolini in Brodo

SERVES 4 | PREP 45 MIN | COOK 30 MIN

Anolini are tiny ravioli—about 1 inch in diameter—that are usually made around Christmas in Parma. It can take three days to make the filling of braised meats and then the broth. This version uses a cheese filling and a quick, tasty broth my mother used to make to cure my colds when I was little.

TOOLS

Stockpot

Tools for Gluten-Free Pasta Dough (page 35)

Rolling pin

Anolini stamp or bottlecap

FOR THE BRODO

1 tablespoon olive oil	32 ounces chicken broth	Salt and pepper
½ cup finely minced carrot	1 (2-inch) Parmesan rind	¼ cup grated Parmesan

1. **PREP.** In a large stockpot with the oil over medium heat, cook the carrot until softened, 5 to 6 minutes.

2. **SIMMER.** Add the broth and Parmesan rind, season with salt and pepper, and bring to a simmer. Cover and let simmer, stirring often, while you make the anolini.

FOR THE ANOLINI

1 Gluten-Free Pasta Dough recipe (page 35)	1 cup grated Parmesan	1 large egg yolk
¼ cup whole-milk ricotta	½ cup panko breadcrumbs	Pinch nutmeg
		Salt and pepper

1. **MAKE THE DOUGH.** Make the Gluten-Free Pasta Dough.

2. **CREATE THE FILLING.** In a large bowl, mix the ricotta, Parmesan, panko, egg yolk, and nutmeg until a thick paste forms. Season with salt and pepper.

3. **THIN, FILL, AND CUT.** Use a rolling pin to roll out two sheets of dough 1/16 inch thick. Spoon 1 teaspoon of the filling 1 inch apart across the sheet. Cover with a second pasta sheet. Use your fingers to push the air out around each knob of filling. Using the stamp, cut out the anolini.

4. **COOK.** Bring the brodo to a boil, remove the cheese rind, and add the anolini in batches to simmer 3 to 4 minutes. Ladle the batches into bowls with a little of the brodo, and top with the grated Parmesan.

> **TIP:** If you don't have a Parmesan rind, you can add ¼ cup grated Parmesan to the broth at the very end. It will make the brodo a little cloudy, but it will still taste great.

Gluten-Free Cannelloni Lucchese

SERVES 4 | PREP 30 MIN | COOK 30 MIN

This recipe was inspired by the filling for tordelli Lucchese—a ravioli with a spiced meat filling from Lucca in Tuscany. After some preparation, this dish bakes while you pour yourself some wine.

TOOLS

Tools for Gluten-Free Pasta Dough (page 35)

Large sauté pan

Large bowl

Rolling pin

Knife

Large stockpot

Baking dish

FOR THE CANNELLONI

1 Gluten-Free Pasta Dough recipe (page 35)

½ pound ground pork

½ pound ground beef

Salt and pepper

1 tablespoon chopped herbs

½ cup chopped onion

½ cup diced salami or pancetta

¼ teaspoon nutmeg

½ teaspoon cinnamon

2 tablespoons pine nuts

2 tablespoons raisins

2 cups chopped Swiss chard

¼ cup grated Parmesan

1. **MAKE THE DOUGH.** Make the Gluten-Free Pasta Dough.

2. **CREATE THE FILLING.** Season the pork and beef with salt and pepper and cook in a large sauté pan over medium-high heat for 3 minutes. Add the herbs, onion, salami, nutmeg, cinnamon, pine nuts, and raisins. Stir and cook until the meat is browned, about 8 minutes. Transfer to a large bowl, and remove all but 2 tablespoons of fat from the pan. Add the chard and 1 tablespoon of water to the pan; cover and steam 1 to 2 minutes until wilted. Add the chard to the large bowl and stir in the Parmesan.

3. **THIN AND CUT.** Use a rolling pin to roll out the dough into sheets between ⅛ and ¹⁄₁₆ inch thick. Use the knife to cut into 3-by-4-inch rectangles.

4. **BOIL.** Bring a large pot of salted water to a boil. Blanch the pasta 30 to 45 seconds before plunging into an ice bath. Drain on a towel.

2 tablespoons olive oil

1 garlic clove, minced

½ cup diced salami

1 (28-ounce) can
crushed tomatoes

Salt and pepper

1 cup grated
Parmesan

1. **SAUTÉ.** In a large sauté pan with the oil over medium heat, cook the garlic and salami 3 to 4 minutes. Add the tomatoes and simmer 10 to 15 minutes. Season with salt and pepper to taste. Set aside ¼ cup of the sauce in a large bowl. Pour half the remaining sauce into a large baking dish.

2. **FILL.** Preheat the oven to 350°F. Lay out the pasta sheets on a board. Place a few tablespoons of the filling on the end of a sheet. Roll up the pasta tightly around the filling and place seam-side down in the baking dish. Repeat until the dish is full, then top with the remaining sauce and Parmesan.

3. **BAKE.** Bake 20 to 25 minutes, until bubbling and beginning to crisp.

> **TIP:** You can use this filling recipe for the more traditional tordelli Lucchese, which are a square-shaped ravioli served with a meat sauce.

Whole-Wheat Pansotti with Walnut Sauce

SERVES 4 | PREP 30 MIN | COOK 20 MIN

Pansotti are triangular ravioli from Liguria filled with herbs and greens. The name is derived from the Italian word for "belly," since these plump raviolis look like potbellies when shaped.

TOOLS

Tools for Whole-Wheat Flour Pasta Dough (page 34)

Large sauté pan

Large bowl

Rolling pin

Knife or pastry wheel

Food processor or blender

Large stockpot

Fork

FOR THE PANSOTTI

1 Whole-Wheat Flour Pasta Dough recipe (page 34)
1 tablespoon olive oil
2 cups Swiss chard
2 cups spinach

¼ cup parsley
1 cup whole-milk ricotta
½ cup Parmesan, grated

1 tablespoon freshly squeezed lemon juice
¼ teaspoon nutmeg
Salt and pepper

1. **MAKE THE DOUGH.** Make the Whole-Wheat Pasta Dough.

2. **CREATE THE FILLING.** In a large sauté pan with the oil over medium heat, cook the chard, spinach, and parsley until wilted, 2 to 3 minutes. Let cool and finely mince. In a large bowl, mix the greens with the ricotta, Parmesan, lemon juice, and nutmeg. Season with salt and pepper.

3. **THIN, CUT, AND FILL.** Use a rolling pin to roll out two sheets of dough ¹⁄₁₆ inch thick. Use a knife or pastry wheel to cut into 2-inch squares. Place 1 rounded tablespoon of filling near one corner of each square. Fold the dough over itself to form a triangle and seal the edges with your fingers or the tines of a fork.

1 slice white bread,
crust removed
2 tablespoons milk
1½ cups walnuts

½ garlic clove
½ cup grated
Parmesan

½ cup olive oil
Salt and pepper

1. **BLEND.** Tear the bread into pieces and soak in the milk until softened. In a food processor, blend the bread and milk, walnuts, garlic, Parmesan, and oil. Season with salt and pepper.

2. **BOIL.** Bring a large pot of salted water to a boil. Add the pansotti and simmer 3 to 4 minutes. Strain, reserving ¼ cup of the pasta water.

3. **SAUCE.** In a large sauté pan, warm the sauce over low heat. Add 2 to 4 tablespoons of the reserved pasta water to thin the sauce as needed. Add the pansotti and stir to coat.

> **TIP:** Pansotti were traditionally made with wild herbs and greens, so you can substitute any variety of either that you prefer—endive, arugula, dandelion greens, etc.

Butternut Squash Cappellacci with Brown Butter and Sage

SERVES 4 | PREP 30 MIN | COOK 50 MIN

Cappellacci date back to the Renaissance. This pasta has an Indicazione Geografica Protetta (IGP) label, which in Italy means a recipe or food that is unique to a particular area, in this case Ferrara in Emilia-Romagna.

TOOLS

Tools for Egg Pasta Dough (page 32)

Sheet pan

Food processor or blender

Rolling pin

Knife or pastry wheel

Large sauté pan

Large stockpot

FOR THE CAPPELLACCI

1 Egg Pasta Dough recipe (page 32)

1 (2-pound) butternut squash, halved and seeds removed (about 2 cups)

½ cup grated Parmesan

½ cup whole-milk ricotta

Pinch nutmeg

Salt and pepper

1. **MAKE THE DOUGH.** Make the Egg Pasta Dough.

2. **CREATE THE FILLING.** Preheat the oven to 350°F. Place the squash cut-side down on a lightly oiled sheet pan. Bake 30 to 40 minutes, until soft. Let cool, then scrape the squash from the peel and blend in a food processor with the Parmesan, ricotta, and nutmeg. Season with salt and pepper.

3. **THIN, CUT, AND FILL.** Use a rolling pin to roll out two sheets of dough ¹⁄₁₆ inch thick. Use a knife or pastry wheel to cut into 3-inch squares. Place 1 rounded tablespoon of filling near one corner of each square. Fold the top half of the square over the filling to form a triangle. Use your fingers to seal the edges. Pull the bottom triangle corners toward each other to a point and pinch to seal.

¼ cup (½ stick) butter
3 to 4 fresh sage leaves

1. **BROWN.** In a large sauté pan over medium heat, melt the butter with sage leaves until the butter starts to foam, 2 to 3 minutes. Turn the heat to low and cook, stirring frequently, until light-brown specks begin to form in the pan, 5 to 6 minutes. Remove pan from heat.

2. **BOIL.** Bring a large pot of salted water to a boil. Add the cappellacci and simmer 3 to 4 minutes. Strain.

3. **SAUCE.** Add the cappellacci to the pan and stir to coat.

> **TIP:** The name "cappellacci" is derived from the word "caplaz," which means "hat" in the local Ferrarese dialect. It's likely based on the resemblance of this pasta to the straw hats worn by peasants during the Renaissance.

Pear-Pecorino Caramelle with Butter and Black Pepper

SERVES 4 | PREP 30 MIN | COOK 10 MIN

This sweet and salty filling combination is popular in restaurants in Florence, and was made more famous when Lidia Bastianich put it on her menu at Felidia in New York City. The caramelle shape is a rectangular pillow of filled pasta with twisted edges that looks like a candy wrapper.

TOOLS

Tools for Egg Pasta Dough (page 32)

Food processor or blender

Rolling pin

Knife or pastry wheel

Large sauté pan

Large stockpot

FOR THE CARAMELLE

1 Egg Pasta Dough recipe (page 32)

2 cups chopped and peeled pear

½ cup grated Pecorino

½ cup whole-milk ricotta

½ cup mascarpone

Salt and pepper

2 tablespoons panko breadcrumbs (optional)

1. **MAKE THE DOUGH.** Make the Egg Pasta Dough.

2. **CREATE THE FILLING.** In a food processor, blend the pear, Pecorino, ricotta, and mascarpone and season with salt and pepper. If the filling is too watery, stir in the panko.

3. **THIN, CUT, AND FILL.** Use a rolling pin to roll out sheets of dough ¹⁄₁₆ inch thick. Use a knife or pastry wheel to cut into 3-inch squares. Spoon 2 inches of filling on the lower third of each square. Fold the dough over the filling. Create a seal by gently rolling the pasta along the table, and then twist each end to seal.

¼ cup (½ stick) salted butter
½ teaspoon black pepper

1. **MELT.** In a large sauté pan, cook the butter and pepper over medium heat until the butter just begins to foam, 2 to 3 minutes. Turn off the heat.

2. **BOIL.** Bring a large pot of salted water to a boil. Add the caramelle and simmer 3 to 4 minutes. Strain.

3. **SAUCE.** Add the strained caramelle and stir to coat.

> **TIP:** The dough needs to be a little wet to seal and twist this shape. If needed, dip your finger in water and run it along the outside edges of the square to seal it properly.

Calabrian Ravioli with Aglio, Olio, and Peperoncino

SERVES 4 | PREP 30 MIN | COOK 10 MIN

These ravioli stuffed with cured meats are typical of the Calabria region. Use any cured meat or salami combination of your choice. Since the ravioli are large, only two or three are needed per serving.

TOOLS

Tools for Semola Rimacinata Pasta Dough (page 37)

Rolling pin

Ravioli stamp or large glass

Fork or fluted pastry wheel

Large sauté pan

Large stockpot

FOR THE RAVIOLI

1 Semola Rimacinata Pasta Dough recipe (page 37)

1 cup diced or grated provolone picante

½ cup Pecorino

1 cup whole-milk ricotta

1 cup minced soppressata or other dried salami

Salt and pepper

1. **MAKE THE DOUGH.** Make the Semola Rimacinata Pasta Dough.

2. **CREATE THE FILLING.** In a large bowl, mix together the cheeses and the soppressata. Season with salt and pepper.

3. **THIN, CUT, AND FILL.** Use a rolling pin to roll out sheets of dough ⅛ inch thick. Using a large, round ravioli stamp or glass, cut into 3-inch circles. Spoon 2 tablespoons of filling onto the center of a circle and top with another pasta circle. Use your fingers to press the pasta around the filling, pushing the air out. Seal the edges tightly with the tines of a fork.

FOR THE SAUCE

3 tablespoons olive oil

2 garlic cloves, thinly sliced

Pinch red pepper flakes

Salt and pepper

1. **SAUTÉ.** In a large sauté pan with the oil over medium heat, cook the garlic and red pepper flakes 2 to 3 minutes, until the oil is infused but before the garlic turns brown. Turn off the heat.

2. **BOIL.** Bring a large pot of salted water to a boil. Gently add a few ravioli at a time and simmer 4 to 5 minutes. Strain.

3. **SAUCE.** Add the strained ravioli to the pan and stir to coat. Season with salt and pepper to taste.

TIP: Peperoncini are little spicy red peppers that thrive in the Calabrian climate. If you can get fresh peperoncini, use one sliced thin instead of the red pepper flakes.

Rotolo with Spinach and Béchamel

SERVES 4 | PREP 30 MIN | COOK 30 MIN

Rotolo, pasta rolls with filling, features the best part of lasagna—crispy, crunchy edges! Try this take on baked pasta for a dinner party when you need to make something with a great presentation.

TOOLS

Tools for Egg Pasta Dough (page 32)

Food processor or blender

Rolling pin

Knife or pastry wheel

Small saucepan

Large saucepan

Large baking dish

FOR THE ROTOLO

1 Egg Pasta Dough recipe (page 32)

4 cups chopped fresh spinach or 2 pounds frozen

2 cups whole-milk ricotta

1 cup grated Parmesan

Salt and pepper

1. **MAKE THE DOUGH.** Make the Egg Pasta Dough.

2. **CREATE THE FILLING.** In a food processor, blend the spinach, ricotta, and Parmesan until the spinach is minced. Season with salt and pepper.

3. **THIN, FILL, AND CUT.** Use a rolling pin to roll out sheets of dough $\frac{1}{16}$ to $\frac{1}{8}$ inch thick. Spread a thin layer of filling onto the pasta sheet and roll up like a jelly roll. Use a knife or pastry wheel to cut into rounds about 1½ inches thick.

2½ cups whole milk

¼ cup (½ stick) butter

4 tablespoons flour

Pinch nutmeg

¼ cup grated Parmesan, plus more for topping

Salt and pepper

¼ cup mozzarella

1. **COOK.** In a small saucepan, heat the milk until warm, 2 to 3 minutes. In a large saucepan, melt the butter on low heat, 1 to 2 minutes. Add the flour, whisking constantly until the mixture begins to bubble, 2 to 3 minutes. Add the warmed milk, ½ cup at a time, whisking until the sauce thickens and is just starting to bubble, 10 minutes. Stir in the nutmeg and Parmesan and season with salt and pepper. Simmer and stir 2 to 3 minutes. Turn off the heat and cover.

2. **BAKE.** Preheat the oven to 375°F. Pour half of the béchamel into a large baking dish. Place the rotolo pieces filling-side up in the dish. Pour the remaining béchamel over the pasta, and top with mozzarella and Parmesan. Bake 30 to 35 minutes, until bubbling and beginning to brown. Broil for 1 minute to crisp the top.

TIP: You can serve the rotolo over a few tablespoons of the Master Tomato Sauce (page 194) for a pretty and tasty presentation.

Tortellini with Burro e Oro

SERVES 4 | PREP 30 MIN | COOK 15 MIN

This simple, two-ingredient sauce of butter and tomatoes is an easy, tasty match for the rich meat filling. The "oro" in the name does not refer to the Italian word for "gold," but is a shortened version of the Italian word for "tomato": pomodoro.

TOOLS

Tools for Egg
Pasta Dough
(page 32)

Two large
sauté pans

Food
processor
or blender

Rolling pin

Knife or
pastry wheel

Large
stockpot

FOR THE TORTELLINI

1 Egg Pasta Dough
recipe (page 32)

1 tablespoon olive oil

½ cup minced celery

½ cup minced carrot

½ cup minced onion

¼ cup diced
mortadella

¼ cup diced
prosciutto

1 pound ground
pork or veal

Salt and pepper

¼ cup grated
Parmesan

1. **MAKE THE DOUGH.** Make the Egg Pasta Dough.

2. **CREATE THE FILLING.** In a large sauté pan with the oil over medium heat, cook the celery, carrots, and onion until soft, 4 to 5 minutes. Add the mortadella and prosciutto, and cook 3 to 4 minutes or until slightly browned. Add the pork, season with salt and pepper, then cook until browned, 8 to 10 minutes. Let cool, add the Parmesan, and blend the mixture in a food processor to form a thick paste.

3. **THIN, CUT, AND FILL.** Use a rolling pin to roll out sheets of dough ¹⁄₁₆ inch thick. Use a knife or pastry wheel to cut into 1½- to 2-inch squares. Place ½ to 1 teaspoon of filling near one corner of each square. Fold the top half over the filling to form a triangle. Use your fingers to seal the edges. Pull the bottom corners of the triangle toward each other and pinch to seal.

½ cup (1 stick) salted butter, diced
1 (28-ounce) can crushed or pureed tomatoes

1. **SAUTÉ.** In a large sauté pan, melt the butter over medium heat. Stir in the tomatoes and simmer 5 minutes, stirring often.

2. **BOIL.** Bring a large pot of salted water to a boil. Add the tortellini and simmer 3 to 4 minutes. Strain.

3. **SAUCE.** Add the strained tortellini to the pan, and stir the pasta to coat.

> **TIP:** For any cured meats needed for a recipe, I ask the deli counter to cut ¼-inch-thick slices for me. Then I use a knife to dice them into the perfect size for many of these recipes.

Gluten-Free Casunziei all'Ampezzana

SERVES 4 | PREP 30 MIN | COOK 1 HR

This colorful, half-moon-shaped pasta comes from Cortina d'Ampezzo, located in the Dolomites north of Venice. Make sure you use fresh roasted beets for the filling: canned beets do not have the right flavor or consistency. You'll top this dish with the traditional butter and poppy seed sauce.

TOOLS

Tools for Gluten-Free Pasta Dough (page 35)

Roasting pan

Food processor or blender

Rolling pin

Ravioli stamp or cookie cutter

Fork

Large sauté pan

Large stockpot

FOR THE CASUNZIEI

1 Gluten-Free Pasta Dough recipe (page 35)

4 whole beets, cleaned

1 cup whole-milk ricotta

¼ cup grated Parmesan

Salt and pepper

2 tablespoons panko breadcrumbs (optional)

1. **MAKE THE DOUGH.** Make the Gluten-Free Pasta Dough.

2. **CREATE THE FILLING.** Preheat the oven to 375°F. Place the beets on a roasting pan, cover with foil, and bake 1 hour until soft. Let cool, peel, chop, and place in a food processor with the ricotta and Parmesan. Season with salt and pepper and blend. If the filling is too wet, stir in panko as needed.

3. **THIN, CUT, AND FILL.** Use a rolling pin to roll out sheets of dough 1/16 inch thick. Use a large, round ravioli stamp or cookie cutter to cut 2-inch circles. Spoon 1 tablespoon of filling into the center of each circle and fold the dough over the filling. Use your fingers or the tines of a fork to seal.

¼ cup (½ stick) butter
1 tablespoon poppy seeds

1. **SAUTÉ.** In a large sauté pan, melt the butter and stir in the poppy seeds. Turn off the heat when the butter is melted.

2. **BOIL.** Bring a large pot of salted water to a boil. Add the casunziei and simmer 3 to 4 minutes. Strain.

3. **SAUCE.** Add the strained casunziei to the pan and stir to coat.

> **TIP:** You can modify the beet-to-ricotta ratio depending on how creamy you prefer the filling. Adding ¼ cup goat cheese to the filling thickens it and gives it a nice flavor.

Whole-Wheat Tortelli with Gorgonzola Sauce

SERVES 4 | PREP 30 MIN | COOK 20 MIN

Tortelli are another type of filled pasta similar to ravioli and are typically square in shape. You'll use a stamp to form the tortelli for this recipe, but you can also use a mold if you prefer.

TOOLS

Tools for Whole-Wheat Flour Pasta Dough (page 34)

Large stockpot

Large sauté pan

Food processor or blender

Rolling pin

Ravioli stamp

FOR THE TORTELLI

1 Whole-Wheat Flour Pasta Dough recipe (page 34)

2 cups peeled and quartered potatoes

1 tablespoon olive oil

¼ cup diced pancetta or prosciutto

1½ cups chopped cabbage

½ cup Asiago or fontina

Salt and pepper

1. **MAKE THE DOUGH.** Make the Whole-Wheat Pasta Dough.

2. **CREATE THE FILLING.** Boil the potatoes until tender, 15 minutes, and let cool slightly. Meanwhile, in a large sauté pan with the oil over medium heat, cook the pancetta 4 to 5 minutes, until browned. Add the cabbage and cook 4 to 5 minutes, until wilted. In a food processor, blend the cabbage mixture, Asiago, and potatoes. Season with salt and pepper.

3. **THIN, FILL, AND CUT.** Use a rolling pin to roll out two sheets of dough ¹⁄₁₆ inch thick. Spoon 1-tablespoon dollops of filling across one sheet about ½ inch apart. Lay a second sheet on top. Use your fingers to mold the dough around the filling to let the air out, and then use the ravioli stamp to cut and seal.

2 tablespoons butter

1 cup heavy cream

¼ cup gorgonzola

¼ cup chopped walnuts

Salt and pepper

1. **MELT.** In a large sauté pan, melt the butter over low heat. Add the cream and gorgonzola, stir until melted, and then add the walnuts. Season with salt and pepper.

2. **BOIL.** Bring a large pot of salted water to a boil. Add the tortelli and simmer 3 to 4 minutes. Strain.

3. **SAUCE.** Add the tortelli to the pan, and stir to coat.

> **TIP:** You can use any type of Alpine cheese, which are firm to semi-firm cheeses made in mountainous regions. They include Comté, Gruyère, Emmentaler, fontina, Asiago, and more.

Corn and Mascarpone Mezzaluna with Basil Oil

SERVES 4 | PREP 30 MIN | COOK 10 MIN

"Mezzaluna" means "half moon" in Italian. You can make the striped pasta for this recipe by combining a basil-flavored dough with a standard egg dough for a colorful variation.

TOOLS

Tools for Egg and Flavored Pasta Doughs (pages 32 and 38)

Rolling pin

Pasta machine

Ravioli stamp or large glass

Large stockpot

Food processor or blender

FOR THE MEZZALUNA

1 Egg Pasta Dough recipe (page 32)

¼ Flavored Pasta Dough recipe (page 38)

½ cup minced basil leaves

2 cups whole-milk ricotta

1 cup mascarpone

1 cup corn kernels

¼ cup grated Pecorino

½ teaspoon salt

½ teaspoon black pepper

1. **MAKE THE DOUGH.** Make the Egg Pasta Dough. Make the Flavored Pasta Dough, replacing the spinach with basil leaves.

2. **CREATE THE FILLING.** In a large bowl, stir the ricotta, mascarpone, corn kernels, Pecorino, salt, and pepper until combined.

3. **THIN AND CUT.** Use the rolling pin to roll out sheets of dough ¹⁄₁₆ inch thick. Cut the basil dough into long strands like fettuccine. Lay the fettuccine in any pattern you like on the egg dough pasta sheet, then press gently with your hands so the doughs stick together. Run the mixed sheet through a pasta machine or use a rolling pin to combine the doughs.

4. **CUT AND FILL.** Using the ravioli stamp or glass, cut the sheet into 2-inch circles. Spoon 1 tablespoon of the filling on the lower third of each circle. Fold the circles in half to make a half-moon shape. Use your fingers to mold the dough around the filling to let the air out, and seal the edges.

1 cup fresh basil leaves   ½ cup olive oil   Salt and pepper

1. **BLEND.** In a food processor, blend the basil and oil until smooth. Season with salt and pepper.

2. **BOIL.** Bring a large pot of salted water to a boil. Add the mezzaluna and simmer 3 to 4 minutes. Strain.

3. **SAUCE.** Spoon a few tablespoons of the basil oil into a shallow pasta bowl, place a few mezzaluna on top, and then drizzle with more oil.

TIP: For a smoother filling, you can blend everything for the filling except the corn in a food processor, then stir in the corn by hand.

Raviolo al'Uovo

SERVES 4 | PREP 30 MIN | COOK 10 MIN

Inside each large raviolo is an intact egg yolk, cooked runny so when you cut into the pasta, the yolk blends with the ricotta and complements the cream sauce. We serve this dish as a first course at an annual charity dinner at my favorite restaurant in Durham, North Carolina: Bleu Olive.

TOOLS

Tools for Egg Pasta Dough (page 32)

Pastry or resealable plastic bag

Rolling pin

Large glass or ravioli stamp

Large sauté pan

Large shallow pot

FOR THE RAVIOLO

1 Egg Pasta Dough recipe (page 32)

1 cup whole-milk ricotta

¼ cup grated Pecorino

Salt and pepper

4 large egg yolks

1. **MAKE THE DOUGH.** Make the Egg Pasta Dough.

2. **CREATE THE FILLING.** In a large bowl, mix the ricotta and Pecorino until combined. Season with salt and pepper. Spoon the filling into a pastry or resealable plastic bag.

3. **THIN, FILL, AND CUT.** Use a rolling pin to roll out two sheets of dough ¹⁄₁₆ to ⅛ inch thick. Cut into 5-by-5-inch squares. In the center of each square, pipe filling into a circle that is 2 to 3 inches in diameter and ½ inch high. Gently add 1 egg yolk to the center of the circle. Lay a second pasta square on top, stretching the dough around the filling. Using a large glass or 3- to 4-inch ravioli stamp, cut and seal the raviolo. Repeat 3 more times to make four ravioli.

½ cup diced
  prosciutto
  or pancetta
¼ cup (½ stick) butter

1 cup cream
¼ cup grated
  Parmesan cheese

¼ cup peas
Salt and pepper

1. **SAUTÉ.** In a large sauté pan over medium heat, cook the prosciutto 4 to 5 minutes, until lightly browned. Add the butter, melt, then stir in the cream, Parmesan, and peas, and season with salt and pepper. Stir and simmer until the sauce begins to thicken. Keep warm. Divide about 1 cup of the sauce into four shallow pasta bowls.

2. **BOIL.** In a large shallow pot, bring 4 quarts of water to a boil. Add 2 raviolo at a time and cook 3½ minutes for a runny yolk. Remove each raviolo with a large slotted spoon and place onto the bed of sauce in each bowl.

3. **SAUCE.** Ladle remaining sauce on top of each ravioli, and serve immediately.

TIP: Stretching the top layer of dough as you drape it over the egg yolk filling is important for the presentation. This will produce a smooth raviolo instead of a wrinkled one when cooked.

CHAPTER 7

Extruded Pasta

Macaroni with Sausage and Peppers, page 164

Extruded Pasta

SERVES 4 | PREP 20 MIN

Extruded pastas—which don't need resting time—have historically been made in factories. But with an electric pasta-maker for the home, or a stand mixer with an extruder attachment, you can make shapes like bucatini, rigatoni, fusilli, and more. Each extruder machine setup is a little different, so review the manual's instructions before starting a recipe.

TOOLS

Tools for
Semolina
Pasta Dough
(page 36)

Pasta
extruder

Sheet pan

INGREDIENTS

1 Semolina Pasta Dough recipe (page 36)

1. **MAKE THE DOUGH.** Make the Semolina Pasta Dough.

2. **SET UP.** Choose a desired pasta shape, and install the corresponding die on your extruder.

3. **EXTRUDE.** Following the directions in your extruder's manual, add dough to the extruder a little at a time. The pasta will start to come out and you can cut the pasta across the die to get your desired length. Continue to add dough to the extruder in small amounts.

4. **FLOUR.** Lay the pasta on a sheet pan, flour lightly, and cover to prevent from drying out; or freeze and transfer to plastic bags for later use.

TIP: If you're using a stand mixer with an extruder attachment, a good rule of thumb is to set the mixer on high speed for long strands like spaghetti and bucatini, and medium speed for short pasta shapes like rigatoni and macaroni.

FEED DOUGH

CUT

FLOUR

Spaghetti al Limone

SERVES 4 TO 6 | PREP 30 MIN | COOK 10 MIN

This pasta in a lemon sauce is quick and made with simple pantry ingredients. Always use fresh lemons, since you won't get the right lemon taste with frozen lemon juice.

TOOLS

Tools for Semolina Pasta Dough (page 36)

Pasta extruder with spaghetti die

Knife

Large sauté pan

Large stockpot

FOR THE SPAGHETTI

1 Semolina Pasta Dough recipe (page 36)

1. **MAKE THE DOUGH.** Make the Semolina Pasta Dough.

2. **EXTRUDE.** Install the spaghetti die, and add dough to the extruder. When the pasta starts to come out, cut it to about 10 inches in length. Continue to add dough to the extruder in small amounts.

FOR THE SAUCE

2 tablespoons chopped hazelnuts

¼ cup (½ stick) butter

1 tablespoon freshly squeezed lemon juice

½ cup heavy cream

¼ cup grated Parmesan

Salt and pepper

2 tablespoons lemon zest

2 tablespoons chopped fresh parsley

1. **TOAST.** In a large dry sauté pan, toast the hazelnuts 2 to 3 minutes, until just browned. Be careful not to burn them. Remove and reserve.

2. **COOK.** In a large sauté pan, melt the butter over low heat. Add the lemon juice and cook 1 minute. Add the cream and cook 2 minutes. Add the Parmesan, stir to combine, and heat to a gentle simmer for 2 minutes. Keep warm while the spaghetti cooks.

3. **BOIL.** Bring a large pot of salted water to a boil. Add the spaghetti and simmer 5 to 6 minutes, or until al dente. Strain, reserving ¼ cup of the pasta water.

4. **SAUCE.** Add the strained spaghetti to the sauce, and stir to combine until the sauce is creamy and the pasta is coated. Add the reserved pasta water if the pasta is too dry. Season with salt and pepper. Top with lemon zest, parsley, and hazelnuts.

> **TIP:** You can use any toasted nut here: pine nuts or almonds work well, too.

Spaghetti Carbonara

SERVES 4 | PREP 5 MIN | COOK 10 MIN

This is probably my favorite pasta ever. I love having friends over for carbonara night, and it comes together quickly after everyone arrives. If you follow the proper technique, you will end up with a creamy sauce (with no cream needed) that coats the spaghetti and doesn't turn into scrambled eggs.

TOOLS

Tools for Semolina Pasta Dough (page 36)

Pasta extruder with spaghetti die

Knife

Large stockpot

Large sauté pan

FOR THE SPAGHETTI

1 Semolina Pasta Dough recipe (page 36)

1. **MAKE THE DOUGH.** Make the Semolina Pasta Dough.

2. **EXTRUDE.** Install the spaghetti die, and add the dough to the extruder. When the pasta starts to come out, cut it to about 10 inches in length. Continue to add dough to the extruder in small amounts.

FOR THE SAUCE

4 large eggs	1 cup diced pancetta or prosciutto	1 teaspoon black pepper
1 cup grated Pecorino		

1. **PREP.** Bring a large pot of salted water to a boil. Meanwhile, in a bowl, beat the eggs and Pecorino until thoroughly combined.

2. **COOK.** In a large sauté pan over medium heat, cook the pancetta until lightly browned, 3 to 4 minutes. (If using prosciutto, add 1 tablespoon of olive oil.) Turn heat to low and keep warm.

3. **BOIL.** Add the spaghetti to the boiling water, and simmer 5 to 6 minutes, or until al dente. Strain, reserving ½ cup of the pasta water.

4. **SAUCE.** Add the strained spaghetti to the pan with the pancetta, turn off the heat, and stir to prevent sticking. Whisk ¼ cup of the reserved pasta water into the eggs. Then pour the eggs into the pan with the spaghetti and black pepper, and stir vigorously until the pasta is coated with sauce. If the pasta is too dry, add a little more of the reserved water. Serve immediately.

TIP: I always add peas to my carbonara. Add in ½ cup of peas to cook with the prosciutto in step 4 and ignore the withering glare of the nearest Italian from Rome.

Spaghetti alla Nerano

SERVES 4 | PREP 30 MIN | COOK 10 MIN

This simple but flavorful dish of spaghetti with fried zucchini was invented by Maria Grazia, owner of a restaurant by the same name in the town of Nerano, just outside of Sorrento. The restaurant still exists today, so you can go and try the original.

TOOLS

Tools for Semolina Pasta Dough (page 36)

Pasta extruder with spaghetti die

Knife

Large sauté pan

Large stockpot

FOR THE SPAGHETTI

1 Semolina Pasta Dough recipe (page 36)

1. **MAKE THE DOUGH.** Make the Semolina Pasta Dough.

2. **EXTRUDE.** Install the spaghetti die, and add the dough to the extruder. When the pasta starts to come out, cut it to about 10 inches in length. Continue to add dough to the extruder in small amounts.

FOR THE SAUCE

3 tablespoons olive oil, divided

3 cups thinly sliced zucchini

1 garlic clove

½ cup shredded provolone picante

Salt and pepper

2 tablespoons chopped fresh basil

1. **FRY.** In a large sauté pan, heat 2 tablespoons of oil over medium-high heat, and fry the zucchini until golden brown, about 5 to 6 minutes. Remove from the pan and drain on a paper towel.

2. **SAUTÉ.** Add the remaining 1 tablespoon of olive oil to the pan, and cook the garlic clove over low heat 2 minutes to flavor the oil. Remove the garlic.

3. **BOIL.** Bring a large pot of salted water to a boil. Add the spaghetti and simmer 5 to 6 minutes, or until al dente. Strain, reserving ½ cup of the pasta water.

4. **SAUCE.** Add the strained spaghetti and the zucchini to the pan with ¼ cup of the reserved pasta water, and stir to coat. Add the provolone and continue to stir until the cheese melts and turns into a creamy sauce, adding more pasta water as needed. Season with salt and pepper, garnish with basil, and serve.

> **TIP:** Cooking the whole garlic clove in oil and then removing it gives the oil a milder garlic flavor. Minced garlic has a stronger flavor than the intact clove.

Pasta al Forno

SERVES 4 | PREP 30 MIN | COOK 10 MIN

Cheesy baked pasta dishes are a dinner favorite, but are sometimes overrun with too much cheese and overcooked, soft pasta. Use a thick, ridged pasta like rigatoni that will stand up to baking while still remaining chewy.

TOOLS
Tools for Semolina Pasta Dough (page 36)

Pasta extruder with rigatoni die

Knife

Large sauté pan

Large stockpot

Large baking dish

FOR THE RIGATONI

1 Semolina Pasta Dough recipe (page 36)

1. **MAKE THE DOUGH.** Make the Semolina Pasta Dough.

2. **EXTRUDE.** Install the rigatoni die, and add the dough to the extruder. When the pasta starts to come out, cut it to about 1½ inches in length. Continue to add dough to the extruder in small amounts.

FOR THE SAUCE

2 tablespoons olive oil	1½ teaspoons minced fresh sage or ½ teaspoon dried	½ cup shredded mozzarella
1 garlic clove, minced		1 cup grated Pecorino, plus 2 tablespoons
Pinch red pepper flakes	½ cup halved Kalamata olives	Salt and pepper
1 pound cauliflower, chopped into ½-inch pieces	½ cup heavy cream	½ cup panko breadcrumbs

1. **PREHEAT.** Heat the oven to 350°F.

2. **SAUTÉ.** In a large sauté pan with the oil over medium heat, cook the garlic and red pepper flakes until softened, 2 to 3 minutes. Add the cauliflower, sage, and olives to the pan, and cook over medium-high heat, stirring often, until the cauliflower is browned, 4 to 5 minutes.

3. **BOIL.** Bring a large pot of salted water to a boil. Add the rigatoni and simmer 5 minutes. The pasta should be a little undercooked. Strain and put in a mixing bowl.

4. **MIX.** Add the cauliflower mixture to the bowl with the rigatoni, along with the cream, mozzarella, and 1 cup of Pecorino. Stir to combine. Season with salt and pepper.

5. **BAKE.** Pour the mixture into a well-oiled baking dish, then top with panko and the remaining 2 tablespoons of Pecorino. Bake 25 to 30 minutes until bubbling and beginning to brown.

> **TIP:** You can use any melty cheese instead of the mozzarella: anything like Asiago, fontina, Gruyère, or even gorgonzola would work.

Bucatini all'Amatriciana

SERVES 4 TO 6 | PREP 30 MIN | COOK 10 MIN

Bucatini is a long, thick, hollow pasta, like a fatter version of spaghetti. This chili-studded sauce, flavored with cured pork, comes from the town of Amatrice, located in Lazio right in the middle of the boot.

TOOLS

Tools for Semolina Pasta Dough (page 36)

Pasta extruder with bucatini die

Knife

Large sauté pan

Large stockpot

FOR THE BUCATINI

1 Semolina Pasta Dough recipe (page 36)

1. **MAKE THE DOUGH.** Make the Semolina Pasta Dough.

2. **EXTRUDE.** Install the bucatini die, and add dough to the extruder. When the pasta starts to come out, cut it to about 10 inches in length. Continue to add dough to the extruder in small amounts.

FOR THE SAUCE

1 tablespoon olive oil
½ pound guanciale, chopped
2 garlic cloves, sliced thin

½ cup thinly sliced onion
1 to 1½ teaspoons red pepper flakes

1 (28-ounce) can crushed tomatoes
Salt and pepper

1. **SAUTÉ.** In a large sauté pan with the oil over medium heat, cook the guanciale until lightly browned. Add the garlic, onion, and red pepper flakes, and cook 4 to 5 minutes. Add the tomatoes, season with salt and pepper, and simmer 15 to 20 minutes.

2. **BOIL.** Bring a large pot of salted water to a boil. Add the bucatini and simmer 7 to 8 minutes, or until al dente. Strain, reserving ¼ cup of the pasta water.

3. **SAUCE.** Add the bucatini and reserved pasta water to the pan and stir to coat.

> **TIP:** Guanciale, cured pork jowl, is traditional, but you can substitute pancetta or leaner prosciutto, which is easier to find. Use 1 to 2 extra tablespoons of olive oil if substituting prosciutto, since it has less fat than guanciale.

Macaroni with Tuna and Olives

SERVES 4 | PREP 30 MIN | COOK 10 MIN

Macaroni, or maccheroni, is a generic word for short tube pasta in southern Italy. It is a versatile shape and can be used with many different sauces. Some extruders come with two die sizes, and I prefer the larger one in this recipe.

FOR THE MACARONI

1 Semolina Pasta Dough recipe (page 36)

1. **MAKE THE DOUGH.** Make the Semolina Pasta Dough.

2. **EXTRUDE.** Install the large macaroni die, and add the dough to the extruder. When the pasta starts to come out, cut it to about 2 inches in length. Continue to add dough to the extruder in small amounts.

FOR THE SAUCE

⅓ cup olive oil

1 garlic clove, minced

2 (5-ounce) cans albacore or yellowfin tuna in olive oil

¼ cup chopped, stuffed Manzanilla green olives

3 tablespoons freshly squeezed lemon juice

Salt and pepper

1 tablespoon chopped fresh parsley

1 to 2 tablespoons lemon zest

1. **SAUTÉ.** In a large sauté pan with the oil over medium heat, cook the garlic 1 to 2 minutes. Add the tuna, olives, and lemon juice and heat through until warm.

2. **BOIL.** Bring a large pot of salted water to a boil. Add the macaroni and simmer 5 to 6 minutes, or until al dente. Strain.

3. **SAUCE.** Add the strained macaroni to the pan, season with salt and pepper to taste, and stir to coat. Top with parsley and lemon zest.

TOOLS

Tools for Semolina Pasta Dough (page 36)

Pasta extruder with large macaroni die

Knife

Large sauté pan

Large stockpot

Whole-Wheat Bigoli Cacio e Pepe

SERVES 4 | PREP 5 MIN | COOK 10 MIN

Bigoli is similar to thick spaghetti, but traditionally made with a torchio or bigolaro. This ancient pasta press design was sketched by Thomas Jefferson while he was traveling through Italy; his patent for a torchio is now filed away at the Library of Congress. You can find a bigolaro online, or use the spaghetti die with an extruder.

TOOLS

Tools for Semolina Pasta Dough (page 36)

Pasta extruder with spaghetti die or bigolaro press

Knife

Large stockpot

Large sauté pan

FOR THE BIGOLI

1 Semolina Pasta Dough recipe (page 36)

1 cup (150 grams) whole-wheat flour

5 teaspoons (25 ml; 25 g) lukewarm water

1. **MAKE THE DOUGH.** Make the Semolina Pasta Dough, substituting whole-wheat flour for half the semolina and adding the additional water.

2. **EXTRUDE.** If using a bigolaro, attach it to a bench, add the dough through the top of the tube, and then turn the handle to push the pasta out of the die. Otherwise, install the spaghetti die on your extruder, and add the dough. When the pasta starts to come out, cut it to about 10 inches in length. Continue to add dough to the extruder in small amounts.

½ cup (1 stick)
  butter, diced

1 cup grated Pecorino

2 teaspoons
  black pepper

1. **BOIL.** Bring a large pot of salted water to a boil. Add the bigoli and simmer 6 to 7 minutes, or until al dente. Meanwhile, in a large sauté pan, heat the butter on low. Strain the pasta, reserving ½ cup of the pasta water.

2. **SAUCE.** Add the strained pasta, Pecorino, pepper, and reserved pasta water to the sauté pan over low heat. Stir vigorously until the ingredients combine into a silky sauce that coats the pasta.

> **TIP:** Pasta water adds body and creaminess to a sauce without using cream. The name of this pasta from Rome means "cheese and pepper," and it is the epitome of simple, but flavorful Italian cooking.

Bucatini alla Puttanesca

SERVES 4 | PREP 30 MIN | COOK 10 MIN

Puttanesca is a spicy, flavorful pasta sauce from Naples. While there is debate as to the origin of this sauce and its name, there is more agreement on the basic ingredients, which include anchovies, capers, olives, garlic, and red pepper flakes. I always add a little olive juice to the sauce for even more flavor.

TOOLS

Tools for
Semolina
Pasta Dough
(page 36)

Pasta
extruder with
bucatini die

Knife

Large
sauté pan

Large
stockpot

FOR THE BUCATINI

1 Semolina Pasta Dough recipe (page 36)

1. **MAKE THE DOUGH.** Make the Semolina Pasta Dough.

2. **EXTRUDE.** Install the bucatini die and add the dough to the extruder. When the pasta starts to come out, cut it to about 10 inches in length. Continue to add dough to the extruder in small amounts.

FOR THE SAUCE

¼ cup olive oil

4 garlic cloves, thinly sliced

½ to 1 teaspoon red pepper flakes

3 to 4 anchovy fillets, in oil, drained

1 (28-ounce) can crushed tomatoes

¼ cup capers

⅓ cup chopped Kalamata or Gaeta olives

2 tablespoons olive brine

Salt and pepper

1. **SAUTÉ.** In a large sauté pan with the oil over medium heat, cook the garlic and red pepper flakes 1 to 2 minutes. Add the anchovies and cook, stirring often, 2 to 3 minutes, until they start to dissolve. Add the tomatoes, capers, olives, and olive brine. Simmer 15 to 20 minutes. Season with salt and pepper.

2. **BOIL.** Bring a large pot of salted water to a boil. Add the bucatini and simmer 5 to 6 minutes, or until al dente. Strain, reserving ¼ cup of the pasta water.

3. **SAUCE.** Add the strained bucatini to the pan and stir to coat.

> **TIP:** This sauce can be made without anchovies for vegetarians (or the timid). To substitute for the briny flavor of the little fish, add 1 to 2 tablespoons of the caper brine.

Macaroni with Sausage and Peppers

SERVES 4 TO 6 | PREP 30 MIN | COOK 30 MIN

This recipe is an adaptation of my birthday dinner at Gocciolina, one of the first authentic Italian restaurants to open in Durham, North Carolina. It's where this pasta-maker goes for delicious pasta made by someone else!

TOOLS

Tools for Semolina Pasta Dough (page 36)

Pasta extruder with large macaroni die

Knife

Large sauté pan

Large stockpot

FOR THE MACARONI

1 Semolina Pasta Dough recipe (page 36)

1. **MAKE THE DOUGH.** Make the Semolina Pasta Dough.

2. **EXTRUDE.** Install the large macaroni die and add the dough to the extruder. When the pasta starts to come out, cut it to about 1½ inches in length. Continue to add dough to the extruder in small amounts.

FOR THE SAUCE

1 teaspoon olive oil
1 pound ground sweet Italian sausage
1 cup chopped onion

½ cup thinly sliced bell pepper
1 (28-ounce) can diced tomatoes

Salt and pepper
¼ cup shredded mozzarella

1. **SAUTÉ.** In a large sauté pan with the oil over medium-high heat, cook the sausage until browned, 8 to 10 minutes. Remove the sausage with a slotted spoon and set aside. Drain all but 2 tablespoons of the fat from the pan. Add the onion and pepper, and cook over medium heat 5 minutes or until caramelized. Return the sausage to the pan, add the tomatoes, season with salt and pepper, and let simmer over low heat 20 to 25 minutes.

2. **BOIL.** Bring a large pot of salted water to a boil. Add the macaroni and simmer 5 to 6 minutes, or until al dente. Strain.

3. **SAUCE.** Add the strained macaroni to the pan and stir to coat. Stir in the mozzarella.

> **TIP:** You can make this dish a pasta al forno by cooking the pasta 1 to 2 minutes less, then pouring it into a baking pan, topping with mozzarella and Pecorino cheese, and baking it at 375°F for 20 to 25 minutes.

Fusilli La Genovese

SERVES 4 | PREP 30 MIN | COOK 2 HRS

This oniony sauce is from Naples, even though it includes "Genovese" in its name. It's thought that the name came from the merchants from Genoa who came to Naples and introduced this sauce. La Genovese is prepared like a traditional ragù, but it is bianco (white), meaning without tomatoes.

TOOLS

Tools for Semolina Pasta Dough (page 36)

Pasta extruder with fusilli die

Knife

Large Dutch oven

Large stockpot

FOR THE FUSILLI

1 Semolina Pasta Dough recipe (page 36)

1. **MAKE THE DOUGH.** Make the Semolina Pasta Dough.

2. **EXTRUDE.** Install the fusilli die and add the dough to the extruder. When the pasta starts to come out, cut it to about 1½ inches in length. Continue to add dough to the extruder in small amounts.

FOR THE SAUCE

¼ cup olive oil

½ cup chopped salami or cured meat

1½ pounds onions, finely minced

½ cup finely minced carrot

¼ cup finely minced celery

½ cup white wine

1 pound chuck roast

Salt and pepper

1. **SAUTÉ.** In a large Dutch oven with the oil over medium-high heat, brown the salami 3 to 4 minutes. Add the onion, carrot, and celery and cook 5 minutes, stirring often. Add the wine and chuck roast, season with salt and pepper, and bring to a simmer. Reduce the heat to low, cover, and cook 2 hours, or until the beef starts to fall apart with a fork. Turn off heat and let cool until you can shred the beef into the sauce. Keep the sauce warm while the pasta cooks.

2. **BOIL.** Bring a large pot of salted water to a boil. Add the fusilli and simmer 5 to 6 minutes, or until al dente. Strain.

3. **SAUCE.** Add the fusilli to sauce, and stir to coat.

> **TIP:** This will make a lot of sauce and it tastes great the next day, too. Try spooning it over potatoes or even using it as a topping for pizza.

CHAPTER 8

Gnocchi and Gnudi

Malloreddus alla Campidanese, page 188

Potato Gnocchi

SERVES 4 | PREP 1 HR 30 MIN

Light and fluffy, potato gnocchi should be made with a starchy potato: russet or Yukon gold work best. I recommend baking the potatoes versus boiling them, for a drier potato.

TOOLS
Knife
Potato ricer
Pasta board
Pastry scraper
Gnocchi board
Sheet pan

INGREDIENTS

2 pounds russet or Yukon gold potatoes
1 teaspoon salt
1 large egg yolk

2 cups (300 grams) 00 or all-purpose flour, plus more for dusting

1. **PREP.** Preheat the oven to 375°F. Pierce the potatoes with a fork and bake 1 hour. Cut them in half and let them cool slightly. Scoop the potato out of the skin and rice it onto the pasta board in a small mound.

2. **MAKE THE DOUGH.** Add the salt and drizzle the egg yolk and 2 cups of the flour over the potatoes. Using the pastry scraper, fold the ingredients until combined. Then use your hands to gently knead the dough 5 minutes. The dough will be soft, but firm enough to stay together.

3. **SHAPE.** Divide the dough into 6 pieces. Starting at the center of each piece of dough, use your hands to roll and stretch the dough back and forth away from you on the pasta board to form ¾-inch-thick ropes. Using the scraper, cut the ropes into ¾-inch-long pieces. Toss the pieces with extra flour to keep them from sticking. Using the side of your thumb, push down lightly and drag one piece at a time across the gnocchi board. This will imprint the gnocchi with ridges and also curl it around the indentation from your thumb.

4. **FLOUR.** Place the gnocchi in a single layer on a sheet pan, flour lightly, and cover to prevent from drying out; or freeze and transfer to plastic bags for later use.

TIP: If you do not have a ridged gnocchi board, you can use the back of the tines of a fork to roll the gnocchi. The goal is to thin out the piece of dough so the middle will cook when boiled.

RICE POTATOES

FOLD

KNEAD

ROLL TO STRETCH

CUT

SHAPE AND FLOUR

Gnocchi alla Bava

SERVES 4 TO 6 | PREP 1 HR 30 MIN | COOK 10 MIN

This rich dish is from the Valle d'Aosta, the mountainous region in the Italian Alps. Made with local fontina, the stringy cheese sauce gave the dish its name: "bava" means drool in Italian.

TOOLS

Knife

Potato ricer

Pasta board

Pastry scraper

Gnocchi board

Large stockpot

Large sauté pan

FOR THE GNOCCHI

2 pounds russet or Yukon gold potatoes

1 teaspoon salt

1 large egg yolk

2 cups (300 grams) 00 or all-purpose flour, plus more for dusting

1. **PREP.** Preheat the oven to 475°F. Bake the potatoes 1 hour. Cut them in half and let them cool slightly. Scoop the potato out of the skin and rice it onto the pasta board.

2. **MAKE THE DOUGH.** Add the salt and drizzle the egg yolk and 2 cups of the flour over the potatoes. Using the pastry scraper, fold the ingredients until combined. Then gently knead the dough 5 minutes.

3. **SHAPE.** Divide the dough into 6 pieces and form the pieces into ¾-inch-thick ropes. Using the scraper, cut the ropes into ¾-inch-long pieces and toss with extra flour. Using the side of your thumb, push down lightly and drag one piece at a time across the gnocchi board. This will imprint the gnocchi with ridges and also curl it around the indentation from your thumb. Flour the gnocchi to keep them from sticking.

½ cup diced
    fontina

⅓ cup heavy cream
⅛ teaspoon nutmeg
Salt and pepper

¼ cup walnuts,
    toasted

1. **MELT.** In a large sauté pan over low heat, stir the fontina, cream, and nutmeg until the cheese melts and the sauce is smooth. Season with salt and pepper.

2. **BOIL.** Bring a large pot of salted water to a boil. Add the gnocchi and simmer 3 to 4 minutes, or until the gnocchi float to the surface. Strain.

3. **SAUCE.** Add the gnocchi to the pan and stir to coat. Garnish with walnuts.

> **TIP:** You can substitute half or all whole-wheat flour or the more traditional buckwheat flour in this recipe. The gnocchi will be a little denser, but the nutty flavor will complement the fontina cheese.

Ricotta Gnocchi with Pan Sauce

SERVES 4 TO 6 | PREP 30 MIN | COOK 10 MIN

Ricotta gnocchi are my favorite, and more forgiving and easier to make than potato gnocchi. If your ricotta is watery, you may need to strain it over a cheesecloth before making the gnocchi.

TOOLS

Pasta board

Pastry scraper

Gnocchi board

Large sauté pan

Large stockpot

FOR THE GNOCCHI

1 cup (250 grams) whole-milk ricotta	1½ cups (225 grams) 00 or all-purpose flour, plus more for dusting	½ teaspoon salt

1. **MAKE THE DOUGH.** Combine the ricotta, 1½ cups of the flour, and the salt on a pasta board. Using the pastry scraper, fold the ingredients until combined. Then use your hands to gently knead the dough 5 minutes. The dough will be soft, but firm enough to stay together.

2. **SHAPE.** Divide the dough into 6 pieces and form the pieces into ¾-inch-thick ropes. Using the scraper, cut the ropes into ¾-inch-long pieces and toss with extra flour. Using the side of your thumb, push down lightly and drag one piece at a time across the gnocchi board. This will imprint the gnocchi with ridges and also curl it around the indentation from your thumb. Flour the gnocchi to keep them from sticking.

FOR THE SAUCE

6 tablespoons butter	1 teaspoon thyme	Salt and pepper
2 tablespoons minced shallot	½ cup white wine	¼ cup walnuts, toasted

1. **MELT.** In a large sauté pan, cook the butter and shallot over medium heat until the butter begins to brown, 5 minutes. Add the thyme and cook 1 minute. Pour in the wine, season with salt and pepper, and simmer 3 to 4 minutes. Stir in the walnuts and keep warm over low heat.

2. **BOIL.** Bring a large pot of salted water to a boil. Add the gnocchi and simmer 3 to 4 minutes, or until the gnocchi float to the surface. Strain.

3. **SAUCE.** Add the gnocchi to the pan and stir to coat.

TIP: Ricotta gnocchi can be pan-fried crispy prior to adding to the sauce. After boiling, add to a separate pan with 1 or 2 tablespoons of oil or butter, and sauté over medium heat until browned.

Spinach Gnocchi Skillet with Vegetables

SERVES 4 TO 6 | PREP 30 MIN | COOK 10 MIN

Gnocchi dough can be flavored with any of your favorite herbs or spices. I like to use spinach for the vibrant green color, but try basil for a summery flavor or pureed roasted beets in the winter for a bright red color.

TOOLS

Pasta board

Pastry scraper

Gnocchi board

Large stockpot

Large sauté pan

FOR THE GNOCCHI

1 cup (250 grams) whole-milk ricotta

½ cup minced fresh spinach

1½ cups (225 grams) 00 or all-purpose flour, plus more for dusting

½ teaspoon salt

1. **MAKE THE DOUGH.** Combine the ricotta, spinach, 1½ cups of the flour, and salt on the pasta board. Using the pastry scraper, fold the ingredients until combined. Then use your hands to gently knead the dough 5 minutes. The dough will be soft, but firm enough to stay together.

2. **SHAPE.** Divide the dough into 6 pieces and form the pieces into ¾-inch-thick ropes. Using the scraper, cut the ropes into ¾-inch-long pieces and toss with extra flour. Using the side of your thumb, push down lightly and drag one piece at a time across the gnocchi board. This will imprint the gnocchi with ridges and also curl it around the indentation from your thumb. Flour the gnocchi to keep them from sticking.

1 tablespoon olive oil

½ cup minced onion

½ cup corn

½ cup peas

½ small zucchini,
  sliced and quartered

¼ cup Parmesan

Salt and pepper

1 to 2 tablespoons
  lemon zest

1. **COOK.** In a large sauté pan with the oil over medium heat, cook the onion until soft, 5 minutes. Add the corn, peas, and zucchini, and cook until the vegetables soften and begin to caramelize, 5 minutes. Stir in the Parmesan, and season with salt and pepper.

2. **BOIL.** Bring a large pot of salted water to a boil. Add the gnocchi and simmer 3 to 4 minutes, or until the gnocchi float to the surface. Strain.

3. **SAUCE.** Add the gnocchi to the pan, and stir to combine. Garnish with lemon zest.

> **TIP:** When using herbs or purees to flavor the dough, you may need to add more flour to counter the extra moisture. Add 1 tablespoon at a time until the dough is no longer sticky.

Basil Gnocchi alla Sorrentina

SERVES 4 | PREP 30 MIN | COOK 10 MIN

Gnocchi alla Sorrentina is a baked gnocchi dish made with tomato sauce and lots of melty cheese. This comes from Sorrento, a town on the Amalfi coast in Southern Italy.

TOOLS

Pasta board

Pastry scraper

Gnocchi board

Large sauté pan

Large stockpot

Large baking dish

FOR THE GNOCCHI

1 cup (250 grams) whole-milk ricotta

½ cup fresh basil, minced

1½ cups (225 grams) 00 or all-purpose flour, plus more for dusting

½ teaspoon salt

1. **MAKE THE DOUGH.** Combine the ricotta, basil, 1½ cups of the flour, and salt on a pasta board. Using the pastry scraper, fold the ingredients until combined. Then use your hands to gently knead the dough 5 minutes. The dough will be soft, but firm enough to stay together.

2. **SHAPE.** Divide the dough into 6 pieces and form the pieces into ¾-inch-thick ropes. Using the scraper, cut the ropes into ¾-inch-long pieces and toss with extra flour. Using the side of your thumb, push down lightly and drag one piece at a time across the gnocchi board. This will imprint the gnocchi with ridges and also curl it around the indentation from your thumb. Flour the gnocchi to keep them from sticking.

FOR THE SAUCE

¼ cup olive oil

2 garlic cloves, minced

¼ cup minced onion

1 (28-ounce) can diced tomatoes

Salt and pepper

¾ cup shredded mozzarella

½ cup grated Pecorino

1. **COOK.** Preheat the oven to 375°F. Meanwhile, in a large sauté pan with the oil over medium heat, cook the garlic and onions until the onions are soft, 5 minutes. Add the tomatoes and cook over medium-high heat, 10 to 15 minutes. Season with salt and pepper.

2. **BOIL.** Bring a large pot of salted water to a boil. Add the gnocchi and simmer 3 to 4 minutes, or until the gnocchi float to the surface. Strain.

3. **SAUCE.** Turn off the heat and stir the gnocchi, mozzarella, and Pecorino into the sauce until combined. Pour into a large baking dish. Bake uncovered 20 to 25 minutes, until the sauce is bubbly and the cheese is melted.

> **TIP:** You can add the ricotta, salt, and basil to a food processor if you prefer a more uniform color for the gnocchi. Scrape the mixture onto the pasta board and continue with the recipe above.

Sheet Pan Gnocchi with Roasted Vegetables

SERVES 4 | PREP 10 MIN | COOK 30 MIN

This is a great way to use up your favorite vegetables for any season. You do not have to cook the gnocchi first. Just toss them in oil from frozen or fresh along with the vegetables, season, and bake.

TOOLS
Pasta board

Pastry scraper

Gnocchi board

Knife

Large bowl

Sheet pan

FOR THE GNOCCHI

1 cup (250 grams) whole-milk ricotta

1½ cups (225 grams) 00 or all-purpose flour, plus more for dusting

½ teaspoon salt

1. **MAKE THE DOUGH.** Combine the ricotta, 1½ cups of the flour, and the salt on a pasta board. Using the pastry scraper, fold the ingredients until combined. Then use your hands to gently knead the dough 5 minutes. The dough will be soft, but firm enough to stay together.

2. **SHAPE.** Divide the dough into 6 pieces and form the pieces into ¾-inch-thick ropes. Using the scraper, cut the ropes into ¾-inch-long pieces and toss with extra flour. Using the side of your thumb, push down lightly and drag one piece at a time across the gnocchi board. This will imprint the gnocchi with ridges and also curl it around the indentation from your thumb. Flour the gnocchi to keep them from sticking.

1 medium zucchini
  or squash
1 medium red
  onion, chopped
2 cups grape
  tomatoes

1 red bell pepper,
  chopped
4 tablespoons olive
  oil, divided
4 garlic cloves, halved
½ teaspoon thyme

Salt and pepper
1 to 2 tablespoons
  balsamic vinegar
2 tablespoons
  Parmesan

1. **PREP.** Preheat the oven to 400°F. Meanwhile, slice the zucchini into
   ¼- to ½-inch rounds, then quarter. In a large bowl, toss the zucchini,
   onion, tomatoes, and bell pepper with 2 tablespoons of oil, the garlic,
   and the thyme. Season with salt and pepper.

2. **BAKE.** Add the vegetables and gnocchi to a parchment-lined sheet pan
   (if using frozen gnocchi, toss with the vegetables; no need to thaw). Bake
   20 minutes, stir, and then bake 10 more minutes. Broil 2 minutes to brown
   the gnocchi and vegetables.

3. **DRIZZLE.** Remove the pan from the oven. Drizzle the remaining 2 tablespoons
   of oil, balsamic vinegar, and Parmesan over the gnocchi and vegetables.

TIP: Use any vegetable combo you like, but keep the proportions the
same, which is about 5 cups of vegetables to 1 pound of gnocchi. Don't
skip the tomatoes, which are necessary to help form a sauce.

Canederli in Brodo

SERVES 4 TO 6 | PREP 30 MIN | COOK 10 MIN

These bread dumplings are an example of cucina povera—or "the food of the poor"—from the mountains of Northeast Italy. Made with leftover ingredients, this filling soup is perfect for chilly weather.

TOOLS

Large sauté pan

Large stockpot

INGREDIENTS

1 large egg

1 cup whole milk

1 cup panko breadcrumbs or diced stale white bread

Pinch nutmeg

Salt and pepper

1 tablespoon butter

2 tablespoons minced onion

½ cup diced speck or smoked ham

½ cup diced fontina

½ cup 00 or all-purpose flour, plus more for dusting

2 tablespoons minced fresh parsley or 1 teaspoon dried

4 cups beef bone broth or beef stock

1. **SOAK.** In a large bowl, beat the egg, then add the milk, breadcrumbs, and nutmeg and stir to combine. Season with salt and pepper, cover, and refrigerate 30 minutes.

2. **SAUTÉ.** In a large sauté pan over medium heat, cook the butter, onion, and speck until the onions are soft and the speck has browned, 5 minutes.

3. **MIX.** Combine the speck mixture, fontina, flour, and parsley with the soaked bread mixture, and refrigerate 30 minutes.

4. **SHAPE.** Using your hands, form balls about 2 inches in diameter, pressing the dough so they do not fall apart. The dough will be very soft and sticky. Roll the balls in flour to keep them from sticking.

5. **BOIL.** Bring the broth to a boil in a large pot. Cooking in batches as needed, add the canederli to the pot and simmer 8 to 10 minutes. Place 3 to 4 canederli each into shallow serving bowls, and ladle in beef broth until the canederli are half-covered.

Gnocchi alla Romana

SERVES 4 | PREP 30 MIN | COOK 1 HR 15 MIN

These semolina gnocchi are a great side dish or main course served with a green salad. They are rich, buttery, and cheesy, but do take a little time to make.

INGREDIENTS

2 cups whole milk

½ cup semolina

1 large egg

½ teaspoon salt

¾ cup grated
  Parmesan, divided

2 tablespoons
  butter, divided

TOOLS

Large saucepan

Sheet pan

Cookie cutter or glass

Baking dish

1. **HEAT.** In a large saucepan, heat the milk slowly over low heat until it begins to bubble. Slowly whisk in the semolina a little at a time. Continue to whisk until the mixture becomes thick, then stir often with a wooden spoon until the mixture pulls away from the pan. Turn off the heat. Whisk the egg and salt, and then stir them into the semolina mixture along with ½ cup of Parmesan and 1 tablespoon of butter.

2. **COOL.** On a parchment-covered sheet pan or baking dish, spread the semolina in a thin layer a little less than ½ inch thick. Cool in the refrigerator 30 minutes.

3. **BAKE.** Preheat the oven to 375°F. Using a large cookie cutter or glass, cut the semolina into approximately 2-inch circles. Add the circles to a greased baking dish, slightly overlapping them in one layer. Dice the remaining 1 tablespoon of butter and sprinkle on top with ¼ cup of Parmesan. Bake 25 minutes, until the top begins to brown.

> **TIP:** These gnocchi taste great on their own, or you can serve them on a bed of tomato sauce.

Sweet Potato Gnocchi with Pecan Butter Sauce

SERVES 4 TO 6 | PREP 1 HR 30 MIN | COOK 10 MIN

Roasted sweet potatoes add a nice flavor to gnocchi and are perfect for fall pasta dishes. The addition of ricotta helps keep these slightly sweet gnocchi light and fluffy.

TOOLS

Knife

Pasta board

Pastry scraper

Gnocchi board

Large sauté pan

Large stockpot

FOR THE GNOCCHI

1 large (1-pound) sweet potato

½ cup (125 grams) whole-milk ricotta

1 cup (150 grams) 00 or all-purpose flour, plus more for dusting

1 teaspoon salt

1. **PREP.** Bake the sweet potato at 375°F for 1 hour. Cut it in half and let it cool slightly. Scoop the potato out of the skin and into a large bowl.

2. **MAKE THE DOUGH.** Add the ricotta, 1 cup of the flour, and the salt to the bowl with the sweet potato. Stir until combined and the potato is mashed smooth, then turn out onto a well-floured pasta board. Using the pastry scraper, fold the ingredients until combined. Use your hands to gently knead the dough 5 minutes. The dough will be soft, but firm enough to stay together.

3. **SHAPE.** Divide the dough into 6 pieces and form the pieces into ¾-inch-thick ropes. Using the scraper, cut the ropes into ¾-inch-long pieces and toss with extra flour. Using the side of your thumb, push down lightly and drag one piece at a time across the gnocchi board to imprint the gnocchi and curl it around the indentation from your thumb. Flour the gnocchi to keep them from sticking.

6 tablespoons butter

3 to 4 sage leaves

½ cup chopped
  pecans, toasted

Salt and pepper

1. **BROWN.** In a large sauté pan, melt the butter with the sage leaves over medium heat until the butter starts to foam, 2 to 3 minutes. Turn the heat to low and cook, stirring frequently, until light-brown specks begin to form in the pan, 5 to 6 minutes. Add the pecans and cook 1 minute.

2. **BOIL.** Bring a large pot of salted water to a boil. Add the gnocchi and simmer 3 to 4 minutes, or until the gnocchi float to the surface. Strain.

3. **SAUCE.** Add the gnocchi to the pan, stir to coat, and season with salt and pepper.

TIP: Add 1 teaspoon of cinnamon and 2 tablespoons of brown sugar to the dough for more of a fall spice flavor.

Spinach Gnudi with Lemon-Cream Sauce

SERVES 4 TO 6 | PREP 30 MIN | COOK 10 MIN

"Gnudi" means "naked" in Italian, and these dumplings are a doughier version of ravioli filling. Made with ricotta and just enough flour to hold them together, these pillowy dumplings are light and tasty.

TOOLS
Sheet pan
Large sauté pan
Large stockpot

FOR THE GNUDI

1 tablespoon olive oil
2 garlic cloves, halved
2 cups fresh spinach
2 cups whole-milk ricotta

1 large egg, beaten
½ cup grated Parmesan
¼ teaspoon nutmeg

½ cup flour
Salt and pepper

1. **COOK.** In a large sauté pan with the oil over medium heat, cook the garlic cloves 2 minutes. Remove the garlic and discard. Add the spinach and stir until wilted, 2 minutes. Move the spinach to a strainer, and using the back of a spoon, squeeze out the liquid. When cool, mince finely.

2. **MAKE THE DOUGH.** In a large bowl, mix the spinach, ricotta, egg, Parmesan, nutmeg, and flour. Season with salt and pepper, and mix until thoroughly combined. Cover and refrigerate 30 minutes.

3. **SHAPE.** In batches, scoop out the gnudi mixture with a spoon, then use another spoon to press and smooth the dough into an oval. Roll the gnudi in flour to prevent sticking, and lay them on a sheet pan. Repeat with the remaining mixture.

¼ cup (½ stick) butter

½ teaspoon
  fresh thyme

1 large lemon, zested

¾ cup heavy cream

2 tablespoons
  freshly squeezed
  lemon juice

Salt and pepper

¼ cup Parmesan

½ cup pine
  nuts, toasted

1. **BOIL.** Bring a large pot of salted water to a boil. In batches, add some gnudi so there's plenty of room between them in the water, and simmer 4 to 5 minutes, until they float. Strain, reserving 2 tablespoons of the pasta water.

2. **COOK.** In a large sauté pan, melt the butter over low heat. Add the thyme and lemon zest, and cook 2 minutes. Add the cream, lemon juice, salt, and pepper, and heat while stirring until the sauce just starts to bubble. Add the Parmesan and reserved pasta water and stir to combine.

3. **SAUCE.** Ladle a few tablespoons of the sauce into a shallow bowl and place 4 to 6 gnudi on top. Top with pine nuts.

TIP: Gnudi are typically served over marinara sauce, but you can use any sauce as a base for the dumplings.

Malloreddus alla Campidanese

SERVES 4 TO 6 | PREP 10 MIN | COOK 20 MIN

Malloreddus are small gnocchi from Sardinia made with semolina flour, water, and saffron, which gives them a bright yellow color. "Alla campidanese" refers to the traditional sausage, tomato, and saffron sauce these little chewy gnocchi are served with.

TOOLS

Pasta board

Pastry scraper

Gnocchi board

Large sauté pan

Large stockpot

FOR THE MALLOREDDUS

¼ teaspoon saffron threads, crumbled	½ cup (120 g) warm water	1½ cups (225 grams) semolina flour, plus more for dusting

1. **MAKE THE DOUGH.** Add the saffron to the warm water, and allow to bloom 2 minutes. Combine 1½ cups of the semolina and the warm saffron water in a bowl and stir to combine. Turn the dough out onto the pasta board, and knead 5 to 6 minutes. Wrap the dough in plastic and let rest 30 minutes at room temperature.

2. **SHAPE.** Divide the dough into 6 pieces and form the pieces into ½-inch-thick ropes. Using the scraper, cut the ropes into ¼-inch-long pieces and toss with extra flour. Using the side of your thumb, push down and drag one piece at a time across the gnocchi board. This will imprint the gnocchi with ridges and also curl it around the indentation from your thumb. Flour the gnocchi to keep them from sticking.

1 tablespoon olive oil

1 pound bulk sweet
  Italian sausage

2 garlic cloves, minced

¼ cup minced onion

1 (28-ounce) can
  crushed tomatoes

¼ teaspoon
  saffron threads

Salt and pepper

1. **COOK.** In a large sauté pan with the oil over medium heat, cook the sausage until browned, 8 minutes. Add the garlic and onion, and cook until soft, 5 minutes. Add the tomatoes and saffron, season with salt and pepper, and let simmer 15 minutes.

2. **BOIL.** Bring a large pot of salted water to a boil. Add the gnocchi and simmer 3 to 4 minutes, or until the gnocchi float to the surface. Strain.

3. **SAUCE.** Stir the malloreddus into the sauce to coat.

> **TIP:** With this dough you can make ciciones, which are a small round pasta from Sardinia. Roll cut pieces of dough into little balls. Cook and serve in the same way as above.

Stuffed Potato Gnocchi with Arrabbiata Sauce

SERVES 4 TO 6 | PREP 1 HR 30 MIN | COOK 10 MIN

You can stuff potato gnocchi with just about anything, from spinach, to herbs, to (of course) melty cheese. The spicy sauce adds a nice contrast to the rich cheese filling.

TOOLS

Knife

Potato ricer

Pasta board

Pastry scraper

Small saucepan

Large stockpot

FOR THE GNOCCHI

2 pounds russet or Yukon gold potatoes

1 teaspoon salt

1 large egg yolk

2 cups (300 grams) 00 or all-purpose flour, plus more for dusting

½ cup (110 grams) fontina cubes (¼ inch)

1. **PREP.** Preheat the oven to 475°F. Pierce the potatoes with a fork and bake 1 hour. Cut them in half and let them cool slightly. Scoop the potato out of the skin and rice it onto the pasta board in a small mound.

2. **MAKE THE DOUGH.** Add the salt and drizzle the egg yolk and 2 cups of the flour over the potatoes. Using the pastry scraper, fold the ingredients until combined. Then use your hands to gently knead the dough 5 minutes. The dough will be soft, but firm enough to stay together.

3. **SHAPE.** Divide the dough into 6 pieces and form them into 1-inch-thick ropes. Using the scraper, cut the ropes into 1-inch-long pieces and toss with extra flour. Flatten a gnocchi piece in your palm, add a cube of fontina, then wrap the dough around the cheese, rolling into a ball to seal. Flour the gnocchi to keep them from sticking.

¼ cup olive oil

2 garlic cloves, minced

1 teaspoon red
  pepper flakes

¼ cup minced onion

1 (28-ounce) can
  diced tomatoes

Salt and pepper

1. **COOK.** In a small saucepan with the oil over medium heat, cook the garlic and red pepper flakes and let simmer 2 to 3 minutes to infuse the oil. Add the onion and cook 2 minutes. Add the tomatoes, season with salt and pepper, and simmer over medium-high heat, 10 to 15 minutes.

2. **BOIL.** Bring a large pot of salted water to a boil. Add the gnocchi and cook 5 minutes, or until the gnocchi float to the surface. Strain.

3. **SAUCE.** Add a few spoonfuls of sauce to shallow serving bowls, and place 5 to 6 gnocchi in each bowl over the sauce.

> **TIP:** "Arrabbiata" means "angry" in Italian, which can describe this spicy sauce. Add as much or as little red pepper flakes as you like, depending on the spice level you can handle.

CHAPTER 9

Sauces, Fillings, and More

Master Tomato Sauce

MAKES 2 CUPS | PREP 5 MIN | COOK 30 MIN

You don't need all day to simmer a sauce—this quick tomato sauce is suitable for any pasta. It's easy to adapt—for example, add your favorite browned meats or vegetables, or use diced tomatoes for a chunkier texture. Longer cook times yield more flavor, but this can be cooked for as little as 10 minutes and will still be better than most store-bought sauces.

TOOLS
Large sauté pan

INGREDIENTS

¼ cup olive oil

2 garlic cloves, minced

½ cup minced onion

Pinch red pepper flakes

1 (28-ounce) can crushed tomatoes

Salt and pepper

1. **COOK.** In a large sauté pan with the oil over medium heat, cook the garlic, onion, and red pepper flakes until the onions are soft, 5 minutes. Add the tomatoes, season with salt and pepper, and cook on high heat until the sauce begins to bubble. Lower the heat to a simmer and cook for at least 10 minutes or up to 30 minutes.

2. **SERVE OR STORE.** Toss with cooked pasta, or refrigerate in a tightly sealed container for up to 3 days or freeze for up to 1 month.

TRY IT WITH: Black Pepper Linguine (page 54), Cavatelli (page 106), Whole-Wheat Pansotti (page 126), Rotolo (page 134), and Spinach Gnudi (page 186).

Sun-Dried Tomato Pesto

MAKES 1¼ CUPS | PREP 5 MIN

This bright red pesto flecked with basil is easy to make and goes well with almost any pasta. To store, add a layer of oil on top and seal tightly in a jar. If you prefer your pesto thinner, add a few more tablespoons of olive oil. You can replace the pine nuts with almonds, walnuts, or pecans.

INGREDIENTS

1 (10-ounce) jar oil-packed sun-dried tomatoes

2 garlic cloves

½ cup fresh basil

⅓ cup pine nuts

¼ cup grated Parmesan

Salt and pepper

TOOLS

Food processor or blender

Spatula

1. **PUREE.** In a food processor, blend the tomatoes and their oil, garlic, basil, pine nuts, and Parmesan for 30 to 45 seconds, until all the ingredients are combined into a smooth sauce. Season with salt and pepper.

2. **SERVE OR STORE.** Toss with cooked pasta, or store in a tightly sealed jar topped with olive oil for up to 2 weeks.

TRY IT WITH: Tagliatelle (page 42), Busiate (page 87), Corn and Mascarpone Mezzaluna (page 142), and Ricotta Gnocchi (page 174).

Butternut Squash Sauce

MAKES 2 CUPS | PREP 10 MIN | COOK 45 MIN

This sauce works well with long-cut pastas like fettuccine. Spice up this creamy sauce to give it the flavors of fall by adding ½ tablespoon of cinnamon and a pinch of nutmeg.

TOOLS

Knife

Cutting board

Sheet pan

Food processor or blender

Spatula

INGREDIENTS

1 (1-pound) whole butternut squash

1 tablespoon olive oil

2 garlic cloves, peeled and halved

1 medium onion, quartered

¼ cup grated Parmesan

½ cup heavy cream

Salt and pepper

1. **ROAST.** Preheat the oven to 425°F. Halve the butternut squash, scoop out the seeds, rub the oil on the cut halves, and place them face-down on a parchment-lined sheet pan with the garlic and onion. Roast 45 minutes, or until the butternut squash is soft. Let cool.

2. **PUREE.** Scoop out the squash's flesh and put it in a food processor. Add the roasted onions and garlic, Parmesan, and cream and process for 45 to 60 seconds, until the ingredients are combined into a smooth sauce. Season with salt and pepper. If the sauce is too thick, add up to ½ cup water (preferably pasta water).

3. **SERVE OR STORE.** Toss with cooked pasta, or refrigerate in a tightly sealed container for up to 3 days or freeze for up to 1 month.

TRY IT WITH: Tagliatelle (page 42), Gluten-Free Pappardelle (page 64), Orecchiette (page 78), Spaghetti (page 150), and Burrata Agnolotti (page 116).

Quick Spicy Sausage Ragù

MAKES 4 CUPS | PREP 5 MIN | COOK 30 MIN

Sometimes you don't have all day to simmer a Sunday sauce, and you simply need a quick, tasty ragù. Use sweet Italian sausage if you prefer less spice. Usually the sausage has enough seasoning, so be careful when adding additional salt and pepper.

INGREDIENTS

1 tablespoon olive oil

1 pound ground spicy Italian sausage

1 (28-ounce) can crushed tomatoes

Salt and pepper

TOOLS
Large sauté pan

1. **SAUTÉ.** In a large sauté pan with the oil over medium heat, cook the sausage, breaking it up until browned, 8 to 10 minutes.

2. **SIMMER.** Add the tomatoes, let simmer 20 to 30 minutes, and season with salt and pepper if needed.

3. **SERVE OR STORE.** Toss with cooked pasta, or refrigerate in a tightly sealed container for up to 3 days or freeze for up to 1 month.

TRY IT WITH: Herbed Pappardelle (page 56), Pici (page 80), Capunti (page 100), Gluten-Free Cannelloni (page 124), and Potato Gnocchi (page 170).

Caponata

MAKES 4 CUPS | PREP 15 MIN | COOK 50 MIN

This Sicilian-inspired sauce has the sweet-and-sour signature of the island's cuisine, thanks to the combination of eggplant, capers, pepper, and a touch of vinegar and cinnamon. This will yield a lot of sauce, and the leftovers can be served on bruschetta, pizza, and more. Credit for this recipe goes to my sister, Rita.

TOOLS
Large sauté pan

INGREDIENTS

¼ cup olive oil

4 garlic cloves, minced

1 cup diced onion

¼ teaspoon red pepper flakes

5 cups diced eggplant

2½ cups diced bell peppers

1 (14.5-ounce) can crushed tomatoes

¼ cup capers

1 tablespoon red wine vinegar

1 teaspoon cinnamon

1. **SAUTÉ.** In a large sauté pan with the oil over medium heat, cook the garlic, onion, and red pepper flakes until soft, 4 to 5 minutes. Lower the heat, add the eggplant and bell peppers, and cook 10 minutes, stirring often until beginning to brown.

2. **SIMMER.** Add the tomatoes and capers and let simmer 30 minutes, or until the vegetables start to break down. Stir in the vinegar and cinnamon, and let simmer 10 to 15 more minutes.

3. **SERVE OR STORE.** Toss with cooked pasta, or refrigerate in a tightly sealed container for up to 3 days, or freeze for up to 1 month.

TRY IT WITH: Whole-Wheat Fettuccine (page 48), Anellini (page 98), Cavatelli (page 106), Spinach Gnocchi (page 176), and Gnocchi alla Romana (page 183). Blend it with some ricotta in a food processor, and you can use it as a delicious ravioli filling, too.

Green Olive Sauce

MAKES 1 CUP | PREP 5 MIN | COOK 10 MIN

This sauce can be thrown together while the pasta water boils. Use any combination of olives and herbs to your liking. Just make sure the olive oil has time to be infused with the flavors of the garlic and olives before you add the cooked pasta.

INGREDIENTS

½ cup olive oil

2 garlic cloves, thinly sliced

Pinch red pepper flakes

1 cup chopped green olives

¼ cup chopped fresh parsley or 1 tablespoon dried

TOOLS
Large sauté pan

1. **SAUTÉ.** In a large sauté pan with the oil over medium heat, cook the garlic until soft. Add the red pepper flakes and olives, and cook 4 to 5 minutes, or while the pasta water boils.

2. **SERVE.** Toss with cooked pasta and serve immediately.

> **TRY IT WITH:** Black Pepper Linguine (page 54), Gluten-Free Capellini (page 68), Foglie d'Ulivo (page 102), Bucatini (page 158), and Spaghetti (page 150). Top with Toasted Breadcrumbs (page 204).

Balsamic Mushroom Sauce

MAKES 2 CUPS | PREP 5 MIN | COOK 30 MIN

This creamy mushroom sauce with a balsamic kick will make it look like you slaved away for hours over a hot saucepan. In reality, though, it comes together quickly.

TOOLS
Large sauté pan

INGREDIENTS

½ cup (1 stick) butter
½ cup finely diced shallot
2 garlic cloves, minced
6 cups sliced mushrooms

½ cup balsamic vinegar
½ cup heavy cream
½ cup grated Parmesan

2 tablespoons chopped fresh parsley
½ teaspoon fresh thyme leaves
Salt and pepper

1. **SAUTÉ.** In a large sauté pan over medium heat, cook the butter, shallot, and garlic until soft, 4 to 5 minutes. Add the mushrooms and cook until they begin to caramelize, 5 to 6 minutes.

2. **SIMMER.** Add the balsamic vinegar and simmer over low heat, 5 minutes. Add the cream, Parmesan, parsley, and thyme to the pan. Season with salt and pepper. Stir until the sauce is creamy.

3. **SERVE.** Toss with cooked pasta and serve immediately.

TRY IT WITH: Herbed Pappardelle (page 56), Cavatelli (page 106), Scarpinocc (page 121), Macaroni (page 159), and Spinach Gnocchi (page 176).

Peperonata

MAKES 2 CUPS | PREP 10 MIN | COOK 50 MIN

This sauce features sweet bell peppers stewed with tomatoes, garlic, and onion. The peperonata takes care of itself, simmering on the stovetop until the peppers break down into a thick sauce. Aside from topping pasta, this is great on bruschetta or with grilled sausages.

INGREDIENTS

2 tablespoons olive oil

2 garlic cloves, minced

1 cup sliced red onion

2 cups sliced
  bell peppers

1 (14.5-ounce) can
  crushed tomatoes

1 tablespoon minced
  fresh basil

½ teaspoon
  dried oregano

1½ teaspoons red
  wine vinegar

Salt and pepper

TOOLS
Large
sauté pan

1. **SAUTÉ.** In a large sauté pan with the oil over medium heat, cook the garlic and onions until soft, 5 minutes. Add the bell peppers, and sauté until soft, about 20 minutes.

2. **SIMMER.** Lower the heat and add the tomatoes, basil, oregano, and vinegar. Season with salt and pepper, and let simmer 30 to 45 minutes until the peppers start to break down.

3. **SERVE OR STORE.** Toss with cooked pasta, or refrigerate in a tightly sealed container for up to 3 days.

> **TRY IT WITH:** Basil Farfalle (page 90), Fusilli (page 96), Bucatini (page 158), and Stuffed Potato Gnocchi (page 190). Blend it with some ricotta in a food processor, and you can use it as a delicious ravioli filling, too.

Tomato-Parmesan Cream Sauce

MAKES 2 CUPS | PREP 5 MIN | COOK 30 MIN

This creamy, mild sauce pairs well with almost any pasta. Add your favorite sautéed vegetables or greens like spinach, kale, zucchini, mushrooms, or peas to give this sauce more body.

TOOLS
Large
sauté pan

INGREDIENTS

¼ cup olive oil

2 garlic cloves, minced

½ cup minced onion

1 (28-ounce) can crushed tomatoes

Salt and pepper

½ cup cream

½ cup grated Parmesan

1. **COOK.** In a large sauté pan with the oil over medium heat, cook the garlic and onion until the onions are soft, 5 minutes. Add the tomatoes, season with salt and pepper, and simmer over medium-high heat, 20 to 25 minutes.

2. **SIMMER.** Turn the heat to low, stir in the cream and Parmesan, and let simmer 5 minutes.

3. **SERVE OR STORE.** Toss with cooked pasta, or refrigerate in a tightly sealed container for up to 3 days, or freeze for up to 1 month.

TRY IT WITH: Paglia e Fieno (page 51), Gluten-Free Anolini (page 123), Whole-Wheat Bigoli (page 160), and Spinach Gnudi (page 186).

Red Wine Sauce

MAKES 2 CUPS | PREP 5 MIN | COOK 20 MIN

This velvety and colorful sauce is a great use for leftover wine (if that's really a thing). Choose a full-bodied red wine like Cabernet or Shiraz to give this sauce depth.

INGREDIENTS

8 tablespoons (1 stick) butter, divided

3 garlic cloves, minced

½ cup finely diced shallot

Pinch red pepper flakes

1 bottle red wine

½ teaspoon fresh thyme leaves

Salt and pepper

TOOLS
Large sauté pan

1. **SAUTÉ.** In a large sauté pan with 2 tablespoons of butter, sauté the garlic, shallot, and red pepper flakes over medium heat until soft, 5 minutes, being careful not to burn the garlic.

2. **SIMMER.** Add the wine and thyme and season with salt and pepper. Bring to a boil, and then immediately let simmer over low heat until reduced by two-thirds, about 15 to 20 minutes.

3. **SERVE OR STORE.** Toss with the remaining 6 tablespoons of butter and cooked pasta, or refrigerate in a tightly sealed container for up to 3 days.

TRY IT WITH: Tagliatelle (page 42), Pici (page 80), Spaghetti (page 150), and Orecchiette (page 78).

Toasted Breadcrumbs

MAKES 3 CUPS | PREP 5 MIN | COOK 10 MIN

Pasta con mollica, or pasta with breadcrumbs, was my comfort food growing up. This is Italian "peasant food" at its very best, using stale breadcrumbs in a delicious way. Below is a kid-friendly version, but you can also add anchovies with the garlic to make this more grown-up.

TOOLS
Large
sauté pan

INGREDIENTS

3 tablespoons olive
oil, divided
1 to 2 garlic
cloves, minced

2 cups panko
breadcrumbs
1 tablespoon dried
Italian seasoning

Salt and pepper
½ cup grated Pecorino

1. **SAUTÉ.** In a large sauté pan with 1 tablespoon of oil over medium heat, sauté the garlic until soft, 5 minutes. Add the breadcrumbs and Italian seasoning. Season with salt and pepper. Turn the heat to medium and stir until the breadcrumbs start to toast, being careful not to burn them. Turn the heat to low, add the Pecorino, and drizzle in the remaining 2 tablespoons of olive oil while stirring to coat the breadcrumbs.

2. **SERVE.** Toss with cooked pasta and serve immediately.

TRY IT WITH: Reginette (page 70), Pici (page 80), Bucatini (page 158), and Spaghetti (page 150). Use it to top olive-based sauces like the Green Olive Sauce (page 199).

Romesco

MAKES 1½ CUPS | PREP 5 MIN

This tangy roasted red pepper sauce goes well with more than pasta—sandwiches, scrambled eggs, even chicken. No stovetop cooking is required, making it great for hot days, or for wintertime when fresh herbs and produce might be lacking.

INGREDIENTS

6 ounces jarred roasted red peppers in oil, drained

½ cup grape or cherry tomatoes

½ cup unsalted, dry-roasted almonds

2 tablespoons chopped fresh parsley

1 tablespoon olive oil

1 garlic clove

1½ teaspoons red wine vinegar

½ teaspoon paprika

Salt and pepper

TOOLS
Food processor or blender

1. **PUREE.** In a food processor, blend the drained red peppers, tomatoes, almonds, parsley, oil, garlic, vinegar, and paprika for 30 to 45 seconds, until all the ingredients are combined into a smooth sauce. Season with salt and pepper.

2. **SERVE OR STORE.** If serving immediately, toss with cooked pasta, or store in a tightly sealed jar topped with olive oil for up to 2 weeks.

TRY IT WITH: Trenette (page 66), Spinach Garganelli (page 88), Trofie (page 93), Macaroni (page 159), and Basil Gnocchi (page 178).

Fig-Gorgonzola Filling

MAKES 2½ CUPS | PREP 5 MIN

This is one of our most popular ravioli fillings at Melina's Fresh Pasta. Sweet figs and salty gorgonzola combine to make this unique filling for ravioli. Top the ravioli with a brown butter sauce and drizzle with honey.

TOOLS
Food processor or blender

Spatula

INGREDIENTS

1 cup dried figs (or ½ cup fig jam)

2 cups whole-milk ricotta

½ cup gorgonzola

Salt

1. **PUREE.** Put the figs in a food processor. Turn it on and drizzle in up to ¼ cup of water as needed, until the figs blend into a smooth puree. Stir in the ricotta, gorgonzola, and salt to taste until combined.

2. **SERVE OR STORE.** Use to fill pasta, or refrigerate for up to 3 days.

> **TRY IT WITH:** This makes a great ravioli filling. Use this in a more traditional large square or round ravioli versus a tortellini so there is more filling to enjoy.

Pea and Pancetta Filling

MAKES 2½ CUPS | PREP 5 MIN

This is like pasta carbonara in pasta-filling form. Try this in a pansotti-shaped ravioli with a black pepper dough to add more flavor. Frozen peas are okay to use in this filling.

INGREDIENTS

1 teaspoon olive oil

½ cup finely diced pancetta

2 cups whole-milk ricotta

¼ cup grated Pecorino

½ teaspoon black pepper

¼ cup peas

Salt

TOOLS

Small sauté pan

Food processor or blender

Spatula

1. **SAUTÉ.** In a small sauté pan with the oil over medium heat, cook the pancetta until browned, 5 to 6 minutes. Let cool slightly.

2. **BLEND.** Blend the pancetta, ricotta, Pecorino, and black pepper in a food processor until combined. Stir in the peas, and season with salt.

3. **SERVE OR STORE.** Use to fill pasta, or store in a tightly sealed jar for up to 3 or 4 days.

> **TRY IT WITH:** This would make a great filling for Agnolotti (page 112) or Mezzaluna (page 142). Top this with the Master Tomato Sauce (page 194) or a fruity olive oil.

Goat Cheese and Honey Filling

MAKES 3 CUPS | PREP 5 MIN

This filling was inspired by a crostini topping from my favorite panini shop in Durham, North Carolina. The owners of Toast took an early chance on downtown and helped revitalize a new, and now vibrant, food scene.

TOOLS
Mixing bowl
Spatula

INGREDIENTS

2 cups whole-milk ricotta

1 cup goat cheese

½ cup honey

½ teaspoon black pepper

Salt

1. **MIX.** In a mixing bowl, stir to combine ricotta, goat cheese, honey, and black pepper. Season with salt.

2. **SERVE OR STORE.** Use to fill pasta, or refrigerate for up to 3 days.

TRY IT WITH: Cappellacci (page 128), Mezzaluna (page 142), or Scarpinocc (page 121). Top with olive oil.

Sausage Filling

MAKES 2½ CUPS | PREP 20 MIN | COOK 10 MIN

Use this filling in larger ravioli shapes, square or round, and pair with a tomato-based sauce to serve. You can even try mixing this with roasted red peppers to add a different flavor.

INGREDIENTS

½ pound
ground sweet
Italian sausage

¼ cup whole-milk
ricotta

¼ cup grated Pecorino

Salt and pepper

TOOLS

Large
sauté pan

Mixing bowl

Spatula

1. **SAUTÉ.** In a large sauté pan, cook the sausage over medium heat until browned, 8 to 10 minutes. Drain the excess oil and let cool.

2. **MIX.** In a mixing bowl, stir together the sausage, ricotta, and Pecorino. Season with salt and pepper.

3. **SERVE OR STORE.** Use to fill pasta, or store in a tightly sealed container for up to 3 days.

> **TRY IT WITH:** Lasagna (page 74), Gluten-Free Cannelloni (page 124), and Cappellacci (page 128).

Asparagus-Ricotta Filling

MAKES 2 CUPS | PREP 10 MIN

If you can get asparagus year-round at your store, you can make this filling whenever you are thinking of spring. There's no need to cook the asparagus for this filling.

TOOLS
Knife
Food processor
Mixing bowl
Spatula

INGREDIENTS

1 pound fresh asparagus

½ cup whole-milk ricotta

¼ cup grated Pecorino
Salt and pepper

1. **MINCE.** Cut the woody ends off the asparagus and mince the rest in the food processor.

2. **MIX.** In a mixing bowl, stir together the asparagus, ricotta, and Pecorino until combined. Season with salt and pepper and blend.

3. **SERVE OR STORE.** Use to fill pasta, or refrigerate in a tightly sealed container for up to 3 days.

TRY IT WITH: Agnolotti (page 112), Pansotti (page 126), Caramelle (page 130), and Mezzaluna (page 142).

Potato, Rosemary, and Asiago Filling

MAKES 3 CUPS | PREP 25 MIN | COOK 20 MIN

When we use this filling in a stuffed pasta at my shop, we call the resulting ravioli "Italian Pierogis." Sometimes I'll bake the filled pasta in the oven at 350°F with bratwurst, peppers, and onions 20 to 25 minutes until the sausage is cooked through, or just give them a boil and then a quick sauté in butter to crisp up.

INGREDIENTS

1 pound russet potatoes, peeled and quartered

2 tablespoons butter

1 garlic clove, minced

1 tablespoon minced rosemary

½ cup grated Asiago

Salt and pepper

TOOLS

Large stockpot

Small saucepan

Large mixing bowl

Spatula

1. **BOIL.** Boil the potatoes 15 minutes or until tender. Drain and cool.

2. **SAUTÉ.** In a small saucepan over low heat, cook the butter, garlic, and rosemary until the butter is melted and the garlic is soft but not browned, 7 to 8 minutes.

3. **MIX.** In a large mixing bowl, mash the potatoes, then stir together with the Asiago and butter mixture. Season with salt and pepper.

4. **SERVE OR STORE.** Use to fill pasta, or refrigerate in a tightly sealed container for up to 3 days.

TRY IT WITH: Ravioli (page 110), Culurgiones (page 119), and Cappellacci (page 128).

Measurement Conversions

VOLUME EQUIVALENTS

	U.S. STANDARD	U.S. STANDARD (OUNCES)	METRIC (APPROXIMATE)
LIQUID	2 tablespoons	1 fl. oz.	30 mL
	¼ cup	2 fl. oz.	60 mL
	½ cup	4 fl. oz.	120 mL
	1 cup	8 fl. oz.	240 mL
	1½ cups	12 fl. oz.	355 mL
	2 cups or 1 pint	16 fl. oz.	475 mL
	4 cups or 1 quart	32 fl. oz.	1 L
	1 gallon	128 fl. oz.	4 L
DRY	⅛ teaspoon	—	0.5 mL
	¼ teaspoon	—	1 mL
	½ teaspoon	—	2 mL
	¾ teaspoon	—	4 mL
	1 teaspoon	—	5 mL
	1 tablespoon	—	15 mL
	¼ cup	—	59 mL
	⅓ cup	—	79 mL
	½ cup	—	118 mL
	⅔ cup	—	156 mL
	¾ cup	—	177 mL
	1 cup	—	235 mL
	2 cups or 1 pint	—	475 mL
	3 cups	—	700 mL
	4 cups or 1 quart	—	1 L
	½ gallon	—	2 L
	1 gallon	—	4 L

OVEN TEMPERATURES

FAHRENHEIT	CELSIUS (APPROXIMATE)
250°F	120°C
300°F	150°C
325°F	165°C
350°F	180°C
375°F	190°C
400°F	200°C
425°F	220°C
450°F	230°C

WEIGHT EQUIVALENTS

U.S. STANDARD	METRIC (APPROXIMATE)
½ ounce	15 g
1 ounce	30 g
2 ounces	60 g
4 ounces	115 g
8 ounces	225 g
12 ounces	340 g
16 ounces or 1 pound	455 g

Resources

Bluone in Italy Food & Wine Tours

Bluone.com
Marcello and Raffaella Tori share their love of Italian culture and its gastronomic variety
through their food-focused tours through different regions of Italy.

Fante's Kitchen Shop

Fantes.com
Fante's is a great source of kitchen utensils for both professional and home chefs. It's a
family-run business that's been open in Philadelphia's historic Italian market since 1906.

Memorie di Angelina

MemorieDiAngelina.com
A beautiful blog with hundreds of recipes in tribute to the author's nonna and
her cooking.

Pasta Grannies

PastaGrannies.com
This website features filmmaker Vicky Bennison's YouTube videos focusing on Italian
nonnas making pasta by hand in their own kitchens.

The Pasta Project

The-Pasta-Project.com
The Pasta Project is a blog by a British expat living in Italy with her Italian husband.
Together, they're working to try every type of pasta available in Italy. The blog includes
so much well-researched information, including recipes for all types of pasta.

Index

Acknowledgments

Thanks to everyone on the Callisto team who helped make this book possible. Special thanks to Lauren Ladoceour, ever-patient editor, for her patience with a first-time cookbook writer.

I would like to thank my family for everything and for all of their support, especially my parents, Giuseppe and Giuseppa, who came here from a tiny town in Southern Italy with my sister, Rita, and brother, Rocco, in tow. And for presenting me to my siblings as a housewarming gift six years later.

A big thank you to Brian Bertolini from Rio Bertolini's Fresh Pasta Co. in Charleston, South Carolina, who didn't try hard enough to talk me out of starting a fresh pasta business, helped me get started, and continues to be my therapy support hotline after 10 years.

To Marcello, Raffaella, and Francesca Tori, of Bluone in Italy Food & Wine Tours, who welcomed me into their home 10 years ago to teach me how to make pasta by hand. I am forever grateful for your kindness and for the pep talk Marcello gave me about starting a business.

I could not have had the time away from the pasta shop to write a cookbook during one of our busiest seasons ever without the hard work and dedication of Sarah Stallings and Greg Courtwright. You both win employee of the week, in perpetuity.

And finally, the biggest and most special thanks to my husband, Billy, for enduring a cookbook-writing process during a lockdown and quarantine when he had nowhere to escape to, all the masked trips to the store, washing endless piles of dishes, tasting almost every recipe, and his love, support, patience, and encouragement for everything I do.

About the Author

CARMELLA ALVARO, owner and pasta-maker at Melina's Fresh Pasta, grew up in an Italian-American family in Syracuse, New York. After years of watching her mother make Italian food with ingredients from her father's garden, she wanted to share in the tradition of cooking from scratch with care and love—serving handmade food to family and friends. In 2010, she traveled to Bologna, Italy, to learn fresh pasta-making. Upon her return, she started Melina's Fresh Pasta, the only small pasta manufacturer in the area. Since then, Carmella has grown the business, opening a retail shop in Durham, North Carolina, in 2017, offering a greater variety of pastas, sauces, and take-and-bake meals to an expanding customer base through farmers' markets, local retailers, and home-delivery companies.